Connecting Washington and China

From Florian Koenigs to AP f
8 - 17 - 19

Connecting Washington and China

✦

—The Story of The Washington State China Relations Council

Wendy Liu

iUniverse, Inc.

New York   Bloomington

Connecting Washington and China
—The Story of The Washington State China Relations Council

iUniverse books may be ordered through booksellers or by contacting:

iUniverse
1663 Liberty Drive
Bloomington, IN 47403
www.iuniverse.com
1-800-Authors (1-800-288-4677)

ISBN: 978-0-595-37510-3 (pbk)
ISBN: 978-0-595-81903-4 (ebk)

Printed in the United States of America

To my mother,
the strongest woman I have ever known.
Her work in China's foreign affairs and foreign trade also influenced me.

Contents

Foreword

Joseph J. Borich

President, Washington State China Relations Council

As a relatively junior Foreign Service Officer working on the State Department's China Desk in 1978, I found myself in an ideal "fly-on-the-wall" situation from which to observe and peripherally contribute to the chain of events that would lead to the full normalization of relations between the U.S. and China on January 1, 1979.

By January 1980, I was in China helping to reopen the U.S. consulate general there after a 30-year hiatus. Although I did not imagine it at the time, I would spend much of the final 17 years of my Foreign Service career involved with China. During that time I encountered the Washington State China Relations Council – its executive directors, board members, member company representatives and delegates of various WSCRC-led missions – on a number of occasions. In the process my knowledge of and respect for the WSCRC and its mission grew with each passing year.

Perhaps it was destiny that the WSCRC's executive director position should become vacant in 1997 at the same time that I retired from the Foreign Service. Whether by fate or coincidence I was ineluctably drawn to accept the Council's offer of employment, an acceptance that years later I have found no reason to regret.

Washington is one of only a handful of states that have found compelling reasons to establish and support a China-centric nonprofit business association like the WSCRC, and the WSCRC remains the oldest and arguably best known of these. The foresight of the WSCRC's founders tying together Washington state's historical links to China with the suddenly unleashed but still not well understood new opportunities for business with China on a massive scale has been fully justified by history. Today Washington leads all states on a per capita basis in trade with China and is the only state to maintain a trade surplus with China. This is very important because no other state is nearly as dependent on foreign trade as Washington – nearly one job in three here is directly tied to international trade. The vision of the WSCRC's founders in 1979 has withstood the test of time.

I congratulate Wendy Liu for writing *Connecting Washington and China*, published originally in 2005, and for updating it with new content. The Washington State China Relations Council has in more than a quarter century become an institution in the state of Washington and in the realm of post-normalization U.S.-China relations. As such, its story is certainly worth telling. But, this work also reflects an intensely personal voyage of discovery for Ms. Liu, with her own metamorphosis on her journey from China to the United States and from normalization through Tiananmen and beyond. That, too, is a story worth telling.

Seattle, November 2009

Opening Note

I am putting together this unique story because I am a U.S.-China relationship buff, and I never came across any story that I wanted to write about so much and could until this one, which, although regional in nature, has all the drama of the U.S.-China relations at the national level.

My enthusiasm for U.S.-China relations—the most unlikely and intriguing of all relations—started with Nixon's visit to China in 1972. But I was not involved until 1979.

That year, when the United States of America and the People's Republic of China normalized diplomatic relations, I was a young staffer at the foreign affairs office of the Shaanxi provincial government in China. That summer, I had the opportunity, honor and excitement of working for the delegation of Walter Mondale, then vice president of the United States, who was visiting Xi'an—the provincial capital and my hometown—to see the terra-cotta army of Qin Shi Huang, the first emperor of China.

That was in fact the reciprocal visit of an earlier visit to the United States that year by Deng Xiaoping, then vice premier of China, on his first official tour after normalization. After meeting with President Jimmy Carter in Washington D.C. and touring Atlanta and Houston, Deng and his delegation came to Seattle—the last stop of that historic trip.

At about the time I was working for the Mondale group in Xi'an, a new organization came into being in Seattle, the first of its kind in the U.S. But I wasn't around to know it until a decade later, in 1989, when I arrived in Seattle and visited it. It was the Washington State China Relations Council, a private non-profit organization with the primary purpose of promoting trade and ties between people of Washington state and people of China.

I was awed and fascinated by the mere existence of such an organization, not to say the people and the devotion behind it. For up till then, in my Chinese life, all organizations focused on foreign relations were governmental. However, with the Tiananmen bloodshed casting a shadow over U.S.-China relations, one wondered if this private council on China could survive.

It did, miraculously. In June 2004, I was privileged to attend the gala of the 25th anniversary of the founding of the Washington State China Relations Council. Seeing and listening to the movers and shakers of the Council as well as distinguished guests from both American and Chinese sides, the old feelings of awe and fascination came back.

The outlet of those feelings is this book. The story of the Washington State China Relations Council is really a collection of stories about its people—those who had the vision to start it in 1979 and those who have had the dedication to continue it since.

It is my hope that this story will fill you, Washingtonian or non-Washingtonian, American or Chinese, with the same awe and fascination I felt.

Wendy Liu

Seattle, October 2005

Part I

Founding

Introduction

As the Chinese saying goes, a journey of a thousand miles starts with a single step. The Washington State China Relations Council (WSCRC) has traveled a journey of over 25 years. Who took the first single step? Whose idea was it in the first place?

That was the work, or quest, cut out for me—finding the footprints of the Council and tracing the steps back to its very beginning—the founding and the idea behind it.

My first step back, however, started with the present in the form of Mr. Joseph J. Borich, the Council's current executive director. For someone like me from Xi'an, the ancient city in China's northwest, it was interesting knowing that Mr. Borich had a reputation as a Shanghai chauvinist. Borich was, of course, not from Shanghai. He had worked in Shanghai for a number of years, including three as the American consul general there. In fact, Borich was from Minnesota, which had a sister-state relationship with Shaanxi Province, of which Xi'an is the capital. That fact, I guess, helped offset a potential Chinese regional tension between us.

When I told Borich about my idea of putting together a history of the Council as an independent project, he welcomed it. In his 2004 year-end newsletter, he informed the Council's Executive Committee and the members this way:

> As most of our readers are aware, the WSCRC celebrated its 25th anniversary this year. Long-time Council fan and essayist Liu Wen has agreed to draft a history of the Council, using remaining Council records and interviews with key figures that have played prominent roles during the Council's quarter-century existence. Some of you may receive e-mails or phone calls from Ms. Liu during the next several months regarding the Council and your involvement in it. If you do, please be assured it is for a good cause, one with my full endorsement.

That was a nice endorsement. I liked it, especially where he mentioned me as being a long-time Council fan. I really was. As for the essayist part, I was flattered. "Essayist" was something I had tried to be on and off since my days in Shenzhen, China, in the mid 1980s.

Anyway, with Borich's endorsement, I was going to have free access to the archives of the Council in its office on the fourth floor of the World Trade Center Seattle, a beautiful blue glass building on Alaskan Way. Entering the office, one's eyes were automatically drawn to Elliott Bay outside the window, with orange cranes decorating the edge of the water. One was also strongly reminded, especially if a train of double-stacked containers went by the building, that this was Seattle's seaport country, the starting point of Washington state's trade with China and other countries. The sign outside the Council office was another reminder, showing two other trade organizations next to the Council.

"The number is 440." Borich was pointing out the suite number to me, pronouncing the digits in Chinese: si si ling, with a little wry smile. I knew exactly what he meant, with 4 being the unlucky number in Chinese culture. Since 8 was lucky, I replied, "You've got to add them up!"

World Trade Center Seattle, 2200 Alaskan Way, Suite 440
Seattle, WA 98121–1684 USA

1.1

Deng Xiaoping in Seattle—The Catalyst

In the drawers containing the Council records, I found a copy of the Articles of Incorporation of the Washington State China Relations Council. Its date of filing with the Secretary of State of the State of Washington was August 6, 1979. Good choice, the eighth month and sixth day, with lucky sounds in Chinese for prosperity and smoothness.

August 1979 was seven months after the normalization of diplomatic relations on January 1, 1979, between the United States and the People's Republic of China. No doubt normalization had provided the historical backdrop for the birth of the Council. But there could have been a number of councils like this one in the United States. Why was there only a Washington State China Relations Council, and not a California or New York State China Relations Council?

What was it that led to a Washington State China Relations Council? It had to be the 1979 visit to Seattle, Washington by Deng Xiaoping, then Vice Premier of China.

I knew about the visit, but not in detail. What did Deng do in Seattle? Who received him? How did the visit go? Was there a link between the visit and the Council? There were so many questions. I had a Deng-in-Seattle-info-treasure-hunt.

After checking around, I zeroed the hunt in on the Seattle Public Library. Although its brand-new futuristic architecture looked a little unbalanced, it had on its 7th floor perhaps the oldest newspapers on microfiche, with the Seattle Times going as far back as 1900 and Seattle Post-Intelligencer to 1876!

With a number of hours over a couple of trips there combing the microfiche, and with repeated excitement spotting pieces of the treasure—headlines, photos, even a banner in Chinese—I selected and copied about 100 pages of write-ups in the Seattle Times and Seattle Post-Intelligencer on the Deng visit in early February of 1979. It was truly a joy reading.

Talk about the Chinese banner which read "Welcome to Seattle, Vice Premier Deng of the People's Republic of China,"[1] I heard an anecdote: Seattle Post-Intelligencer

---

1.   Seattle Post-Intelligencer, Commemorative Edition, Feb. 3, 1979

hired someone to write it in Chinese characters. The characters, however, turned out to be in the traditional style that was no longer widely used in China. P-I could not read or tell. Well, It's the thought that counts.

The following is my abridged version of the visit that I believe served as the catalyst of the birth of the Washington State China Relations Council.

5: 40 pm, Feb. 3, 1979, Saturday, it was slightly chilly in Seattle when Deng Xiaoping—then Vice Premier of People's Republic of China—arrived at Boeing Field aboard President Jimmy Carter's Air Force One. With him was his wife Zhuo Lin, Chinese Foreign Affairs Minister Huang Hua, Chinese Foreign Trade Minister Li Qiang and nearly 100 Chinese officials and journalists. Among those who flew in with Mr. Deng from Houston were then Transportation Secretary Brock Adams, Agriculture Secretary Robert Bergland, the United States Ambassador designate to China Leonard Woodcock, China's Ambassador to the United States Chai Zemin as well as Washington Congressmen Mike Lowry, Al Swift, Norm Dicks, Don Bonker and Tom Foley.

On the ground waiting for the Chinese guests by the red carpet was a welcoming committee led by then Washington State Governor Dixy Lee Ray, with members including Seattle Mayor Charles Royer, Senators Warren G. Magnuson and Henry M. Jackson, and Representatives Joel Pritchard of Seattle and Mike McCormack of Richland. Also waiting were 200 reporters and photographers from various countries who had flown in on separate planes ahead of Air Force One, another 100 Seattle reporters and photographers, and local groups of citizens—welcomers as well as demonstrators.

Governor Ray summed up the moment this way, "It's a very significant thing. It's been since the late '40s since there's been any communication."[2] Sen. Jackson expressed his welcome by giving Mr. Deng a bear hug. Sen. Magnuson rode with Mr. Deng in a black limousine to the Washington Plaza Hotel (The Westin Seattle today) where the Chinese party was staying. The hotel executive chef Karl Hutter that day prepared a dinner of salmon for the Chinese delegation, with tomatoes cut into flower shapes atop as well as other decorations made of crab and olives.[3]

---

2. "'Star and Stripes' for Teng," *Seattle Post-Intelligencer*, Feb. 4, 1979, p. A1
3. Svein Gilje, "Teng begins 40-hour Seattle tour today," *The Seattle Times*, Feb. 3, 1979, p. A4

Next morning, Sunday, Feb. 4, Mr. Deng met in the hotel separately with former Secretary of State Henry Kissinger, Sen. Jackson and a group of Chinese Americans. During the meetings with Sen. Jackson and Chinese Americans, Deng gave assurance that Beijing would open up emigration. Free emigration was a requirement for the United States to grant Most Favored Nation trade status to a non-market economy.

While Deng was in the meetings, part of the Chinese delegation, headed by Foreign Minister Huang Hua, toured the Port of Seattle on a Boeing jetfoil. Wearing blue Port of Seattle caps, the Chinese were shown the port facilities and briefed the port expansion plans. On board with the visitors were Mayor Royer and several members of the Washington's congressional delegation.

Noon that day saw a civic luncheon of 600 people at the Washington Plaza Hotel in honor of Vice Premier Deng and his wife Zhuo Lin. Among them were some of the founders and supporters to be of the Council. Hosting the luncheon were Edward E. Carlson, Chairman of U.A.L., Inc., holding company of United Air Lines and Western International Hotels, and T.A. Wilson, Chairman of The Boeing Company.

Sen. Warren Magnuson said to the Chinese visitors, "It's kinda natural you came to Seattle. We have a lot to offer—trade and transportation. We are closest to the Orient. In fact, we're oriented to the Orient."[4]

In the midst of loud applause, Mr. Deng, dressed in the blue-gray Mao suit, spoke to the audience through an interpreter, acknowledging Sen. Magnuson's statement,

> "The last stop on our journey is this city of yours known as the 'Gateway to the Orient.' This strengthens our awareness of the fact that our two countries are neighbors on the opposite shores of an ocean."[5]

---

4.   Shelby Scates, "Pragmatic Chinese, Practical Seattle," *Seattle Post-Intelligence*, Feb. 5, 1979, p. A3

5.   George Foster, "Teng Tours Seattle And Hails 'Gateway to Orient," *Seattle Post-Intelligencer*, Feb. 5, 1979.

"The Pacific, instead of a barrier, should henceforth serve as a link."[6]

"It is the Chinese people's wish that our two peoples be friends from generation to generation. After our contacts in the last few days with the leaders of your government and with friends in all walks of life, we have the deep impression that this wish is shared by the American people."[7]

"China has embarked on a new Long March whose goal is the modernization of our agriculture, industry, science and technology, and national defense by the end of the century."[8]

"The steady development of Sino-United States relations will certainly exert a positive and far-reaching influence on the situation in the Pacific region and in the world as a whole."[9]

"Although our stay has been short, our friendship is of long duration. May the friendship between the Chinese and American people be everlasting!"[10]

Finally, Mr. Deng proposed "gan bei!"—dry up your cup—to the American people of their continued achievement of new successes. The audience shouted "gan bei!" back

That afternoon, Vice Premier Deng saw something he had looked forward to and enjoyed it very much. With Boeing Chairman T.A. Wilson next to him in a golf cart, Mr. Deng toured the large Boeing 747–767 assembling plant at Paine Field in Everett and watched a huge nose section of a 747 jet carried by an overhead crane pass within 25 feet of him.[11]

Earlier in Atlanta, Mr. Deng and the delegation had seen a Ford Motor Co. plant. In Houston, they had visited the Johnson Space Center and the Hughes Tools Co. oil drilling equipment plant. Now with the tour of the port facilities

---

6.   Svein Gilje and Steve Johnston, "Teng ends historic U.S. visit," *The Seattle Times*, Feb. 5, 1979, p. A1

7.   Svein Gilje, "Teng toasts 'neighbors on opposite shores,'" *The Seattle Times*, Feb. 5, 1979.

8.   Ibid.

9.   Ibid.

10. Ibid.

11. Svein Gilje and Steve Johnston, "Teng ends historic U.S. visit," *The Seattle Times*, Feb. 5, 1979, p. A1

and aircraft plant in Seattle, one could see clearly the strong Chinese interest in American technologies.

That evening, Mr. Deng attended a smaller dinner at Canlis Restaurant, one of the most elegant in Seattle, hosted by local business leaders Robert Ferrie, President of the Intalco Aluminum Corp, Ferndale; John M. Fluke, Chairman of the John M. Fluke Manufacturing Co.; Charles M. Pigott, President of PACCAR, Inc.; Walter E. Shoenfeld, President of the Shoenfeld Corp.; and George H. Weyerhaeuser, President of Weyerhaeuser Co. As one reporter described, "Corporate barons and communist bureaucrats supped in a soft light in the best commercial tradition of people who need each other."[12]

Early morning, Feb. 5, Monday, it was drizzling. Mr. Deng had come down with a cold and skipped a breakfast with the Northwest media executives sponsored by the Seattle Times and Seattle Post-Intelligencer. Still, in his parting remarks at Boeing field, Mr. Deng had warm words to say, "I feel the establishment of Sino-United States relations will firmly impact stability and peace in the world. We feel this visit has been successful."[13] Members of his delegation agreed. They described that the reception in Seattle was warmer than in Atlanta and Houston, despite the slightly blustery weather.[14] Gov. Ray and a delegation of state officials were on hand again to bid farewell to the Chinese visitors. To each "goodbye" and "good luck", Deng replied "We welcome you in China" or "see you in Beijing."[15] At 9:20, the Chinese national Boeing 707 jet took off.

Mr. Deng stayed in Seattle for only 40 hours. But those 40 hours were filled with warmth and understanding of long lost friends of 30 years. Mr. Deng's visit was described as a whirlwind. But the whirlwind left a wake that was long and strong. Riding high on it were new friends of China's and new traders with China, most importantly the founders, directors, and presidents to be of the Washington State China Relations Council.

---

12. Shelby Scates, "Pragmatic Chinese, Practical Seattle," *Seattle Post-Intelligencer*, Feb. 5, 1979, p. A3

13. Svein Gilje and Steve Johnston, "Teng ends historic U.S. visit," *The Seattle Times*, Feb. 5, 1979, p. A1

14. Ibid.

15. George Foster, "Teng Goes Home, Leaves Door Open," *Seattle Post-Intelligencer*, Feb. 6, 1979, p. A1

Deng Xiaoping and delegation tour Boeing 747 assembling plant, Feb. 5, 1979
(Reprinted from microfiche with the permission of Seattle Post-Intelligencer)

1.2

Maggie & Scoop—The Tradition

If Deng Xiaoping's visit served as the catalyst of the birth of the Council, why didn't it do the same in, for instance, Georgia and Texas, the two states Deng had also visited? What was there about Washington state that made the difference?

In the Articles of Incorporation of the Council were signatures of five people, four men and one woman. The first was Robert C. Anderson, followed by Patricia M. Baillargeon, Stanley H. Barer, James D. Dwyer and Richard L. Kirk. I had heard some of the names. But what was the story of each of them? How did they get together in founding the Council? One thing was clear. They were the five leading characters I was going to pursue about the founding of the Council.

Mr. Anderson, at the time of the incorporation, was the Director of the Washington State Department of Commerce and Economic Development. He was also the first president of the Council. Obviously, he was the first person I wanted to interview.

It was in fact the second time I met Anderson. I had seen him first at the gala of the 25th anniversary of the Council in June 2004. When I was told that Anderson was one of the founders, I said they should be called the forefathers of the Council (with one foremother, of course.) Anderson laughed and said he was not that old.

He was right. In 1979, Anderson must have been only in his 30s or 40s. He is still energetic today, and very affable, too. Semi-retired as I understood, Anderson still kept a busy schedule as the Senior Trade Advisor to Snohomish County. He suggested that we meet at the Council office. I thought it was quite fitting. That morning, it was pouring outside. We began our conversation in a warm conference room inside.

What I wanted very much to know, I said, was when and where and from whom came the idea of starting the Council, and whether it was the result of Deng Xiaoping's visit.

The idea came from a number of people, Anderson began. Of course, he said, if Deng hadn't visited Seattle, this whole thing may not have happened. But it was not just because of Deng's visit. It was because a number of things and a number of the right people at the right time and place in Washington state.

There were Senators Henry (Scoop) Jackson and Warren Magnuson, for instance, and their effort in developing relations with China over the years, Mr. Anderson started to count...

Of course! I remembered. Sen. Jackson was from Everett. Mr. Anderson was the mayor of Everett for eight years before taking the cabinet post in the Washington state government. "I was one of the 'Scoop's Troops,'" he told me proudly.

"Scoop's Troops," as I found out, was an informal circle of people in government and business who had worked for Sen. Jackson, and remained friends for many years. As the Mayor of Everett, the hometown of Scoop, Anderson spent a lot of time with the senator, discussing politics, business, or just paying each other visit at home. Anderson was still grateful today, while telling me about it, for the help Scoop gave him in obtaining grants, etc, for his city.

There was...There was also...Mr. Anderson went on...

I got it. The catalyst alone was not enough. Before reaching the point where the Council was born, I needed to look at the people and environment that made that birth possible. I realized that Deng Xiaoping didn't just come to Seattle because of Boeing and the Port of Seattle. He also came to Seattle because of the two powerful, colorful and legendary China-friendly Democratic senators from Washington state.

Described in the online encyclopedia of Washington state history as Washington's one-two punch, Maggie and Scoop were the nicknames of Sen. Warren G. Magnuson and Sen. Henry M. Jackson. In addition to their brilliant service and contributions respectively to the State of Washington by bringing federal funds to various state enterprises from environmental protection to hydroelectric power, from highways to higher education, from public transit to public health, the two had also developed early in their careers of three decades something in common: a strong interest in the normalization of relations of between the United States and China.

Maggie had long cared about China and its people. As soon as he was elected to the House of Representatives in 1937, he started working to eliminate the provisions of the "Chinese Exclusion Act" of 1862 from U.S. immigration laws. That he succeeded in accomplishing in 1965.[16] In 1940, after the Japanese invasion of China, especially the Rape of Nanjing, Rep. Magnuson was instrumental in banning the export of scrap steel to Japan. Scrap was leaving through Seattle and other West Coast ports.[17] Soon after Mao proclaimed the founding of the People's Republic of China in 1949, Maggie began advocating normal relations with China.

Suspected and referred to as a Red and a Communist, Maggie never wavered from his view, "We can't write off 700 million people because they've been united under a Communist regime. We should bring them into the United Nations and make trade—and pacify the Pacific Rim with commerce."[18] As early as 1958, he told Seattle Post-Intelligencer that it should write editorials in favor of trade with China because "the most stupid policy we could follow is to pretend 700 million people in the world don't exist."[19] A famous and mysterious 1973 photo of Maggie laughing with then Chinese Premier Zhou Enlai was perhaps the most poignant image of his friendship with China.

Known as a "Cold War liberal,"[20] Scoop had always believed in strong defense. He insisted that America's self-interest and the interests of humanity were not inherently incompatible. On the contrary, he claimed, the world was a better place as a result of the vigorous application of American power.[21]

---

16. HistoryLink, "Magnuson, Sen. Warren G., and the Relations with the People's Republic of China," http://www.historylink.org/essays/output.cfm?file_id=5524
17. Bruce Ramsey, "In 1930s Seattle scrap steel was a case for trade sanctions," *Seattle Post-Intelligencer*, Jul. 29, 1998
18. HistoryLink, "Magnuson, Sen. Warren G., and the Relations with the People's Republic of China," http://www.historylink.org/essays/output.cfm?file_id=5524
19. Ibid.
20. HistoryLink, "Jackson, Henry M. 'Scoop,'" http://www.historylink.org/essays/output.cfm?file_id=5516
21. Lawrence F. Kaplan, "How the Democrats Became Hawks," *The New Republic*, Oct. 20, 2000, http://www.tnr.com/102300/2kaplan102300.html

Scoop was strongly opposed to any detente with then Soviet Union, either by President Nixon or President Carter. He didn't mind, however, the "détente" with China. He pushed for it. It was his belief that maintaining closer diplomatic and trade ties was the best approach to China.[22] He talked about working out "a livable relationship with the Chinese Communists" as early as 1966[23], traveled to China a number of times from mid 1970s to early 80s, and in fact helped shape U.S. China policy both before and after normalization.

Known for his bipartisanship when it came to foreign and defense policy, Scoop's famous words were often quoted, "In matters of national security, the best politics is no politics."[24] The highest recognition of that bipartisanship came, posthumously, in the form of a Presidential Medal of Freedom and the praise of Republican Ronald Reagan during his presidency: "His sense of bipartisanship was not only natural and complete; it was courageous."[25] It was. The best demonstration of that bipartisanship was, perhaps, his support of President Nixon's China initiative.

Sen. Jackson was also the co-sponsor of the namesake legislation Jackson-Vanik Amendment to the Trade Reform Act of 1974, together with Rep. Charles Vanik of Ohio. The amendment was designed to put pressure on the Soviet Union to end its restrictions to emigration by its citizens, especially Jews, and was extended to all communist or non-market-economy countries. It linked the emigration policy of such countries to the benefits of trade with the United States. Without an open emigration policy, a communist, non-market economy would be denied Most-Favored-Nation (MFN) trade status, or low tariff rates status, from the United States. It would also be denied financial credits from the various organs of the American government, such as the Export Import Bank, the Commodity Credit Corporation, and the Overseas Private Investment Corporation.

---

22. Ibid.
23. UW Libraries, Special Collections, *"Henry M. Jackson Papers."* http://www.lib.washington.edu/specialcoll/findaids/docs/papersrecords/JacksonHenry3560.xml#a1
24. Ronald Reagan, "Remarks on Awarding the Presidential Medal of Freedom to the Late Henry M. Jackson of Washington," June 26, 1984, http://www.medaloffreedom.com/HenryJackson.htm
25. Ibid.

That was the reason why Vice Premier Deng Xiaoping discussed China's emigration policy with Sen. Jackson in Seattle on that February morning. After Deng as well as Foreign Minister Huang gave assurances that China would open up its emigration policy, especially for family reunions, Sen. Jackson immediately announced in a public statement that he would support Most-Favored-Nation trade status for the People's Republic of China.[26] That was probably the earliest such statement from any American politician.

In July 1979, the U.S. and China signed their agreement on trade relations after the normalization of diplomatic relations, extending to each other Most-Favored-Nation treatment. The agreement went into effect in 1980. Due to the Jackson-Vanik amendment of the 1974 Trade Act, however, China's MFN status would remain subject to annual review in Congress for the next twenty years.

I wonder what Washington state's beloved Scoop and Maggie would say if they came back and learned that China is now a member of the World Trade Organization...But I also take comfort in the fact that the two great senators, not only of Washington state, but also of the United States, were both spared the bloody scene of Tiananmen Square of June 4, 1989. Scoop died on September 1, 1983, and Maggie, May 20, 1989

It was most fortunate that Washington state had giants like Scoop and Maggie and the long tradition of building relations with China that they embodied. It was also fortunate that both senators witnessed the birth of the Washington State China Relations Council and helped it grow for a number of years.

---

26. Svein Gilje and Steve Johnston, "Teng ends historic U.S. visit," *The Seattle Times,* Feb. 5, 1979, p. A1

Deng, Scoop and Maggie, Feb. 5, 1979
(Reprinted from microfiche with the permission of Seattle Post-Intelligencer)

1.3

Liu Lin Hai the Freighter and Stanley Barer Who Launched Its Voyage to Seattle

Stanley H. Barer, early 1980s

If members of Deng Xiaoping's delegation felt warm in Seattle on that chilly February day, the atmosphere in Seattle in April of 1979 would certainly have been described as hot.

When the Liu Lin Hai, a cargo ship and the first Chinese flag vessel in 30 years to call on a U.S. port, docked at Pier 91 of the Port of Seattle on April 18, three hundred people were there to greet it. Among them were Transportation Secretary Brock Adams, his Chinese counterpart, Vice Minister of Communications Peng Deqing, who had flown in the day before, our famous one-two punch Sens. Warren Magnuson and Henry Jackson, Chinese Ambassador

Chai Zeming, Governor Dixy Lee Ray, Mayor Charles Royer, Henry L. Kotkins, President of the Port of Seattle Commission, Richard Ford, Port Executive Director, James D. Dwyer, Senior Director of Port Development and Relations, other business and industry leaders, and a group of Chinese Americans. Also greeting the 42-member crew were red banners written in Chinese characters and a Navy brass band blaring the Chinese national anthem and the Star Spangled Banner.

In the Seattle Times, a cheerful cartoon depicted the Liu Lin Hai moored at terminal 91, with the five-star Chinese flag fluttering on top and a banner next to it saying 'Go Sonics!'[27] It must have helped, because the Sonics went on to secure the NBA championship on June 1 that year.

The Liu Lin Hai came without cargo. But she was to load 37,000 tons, $5 million worth, of Midwest corn for its journey home.[28] Its captain, Mr. Bei Hanting, said it best, "We brought no cargo this trip, but we came full of goodwill."[29]

The response of Brock Adams, the Transportation Secretary, was equally hearty, "We hope the ship will carry not only grain but friendship from the hearts of our people back to China."

Mayor Royer had warm words, too, "On behalf of the people of Seattle we welcome you and look forward with anticipation to your visit."[30] He added how Vice Premier Deng Xiaoping had made a real impression on Seattle and how Seattle would make the guests very welcome.

The man in this jubilant crowd with the widest grin was Stanley H. Barer, a handsome 39-year-old attorney, as described by a local paper in its story of the event.

---

27. Brian Basset, *The Seattle Times*, Apr. 19, 1979, p. A12
28. Glen Carter, "Festivities over, it's back to work for Chinese ship," *The Seattle Times,* Apr. 19, 1979, p. E20
29. George Foster, "Building 'a Bridge Across the Ocean,'" *Seattle Post-Intelligencer*, Apr. 19, 1979, p. A13
30. Joe Frisino, "The First Chinese Flagship In 30 Years Arrives Today," *Seattle Post-Intelligencer*, Apr. 18, 1979, p. 3

Barer was not just any attorney. He was the attorney who played the instrumental role in bringing the Liu Lin Hai from China, in essence restarting seaborne trade between the United States and China after a three-decade hiatus. Barer had plenty of reasons to be glowing that day because the Liu Lin Hai arrival culminated four years of his work. It was his brainchild.

First as one of the staff "whiz kids" and later as the administrative assistant, Barer worked for the legendary Maggie, Sen. Warren Magnuson, from 1964 to 1974. He also served as the Transportation Counsel and Acting General Counsel to the U.S. Senate Committee on Commerce during those years.

One might know that Sen. Magnuson went to China in 1973 heading the first U.S. congressional delegation there. But one might not know that it was Barer who had arranged the trip. In those pre-normalization days, Barer had to be in contact with the Chinese government through its embassy in Ottawa. It is also interesting to know that it was the Chinese who had asked that Sen. Magnuson chair the delegation because he was an old friend.

It seemed natural that Barer had been interested in China for a long time. As he told reporters, "You can't work for 10 years in the office of Warren Magnuson and not be a believer in the importance of China, of peaceful commerce with Asia." [31]

It was from that belief that Barer had spent four years working to realize a dream like this—the Liu Lin Hai in Seattle.

In 1949, the year Mao Zedong proclaimed the founding of the People's Republic of China, the U.S. and China respectively froze each other's assets. About $200 million worth of American assets were taken over in China and about $80 million worth of Chinese assets in the U.S.[32] For the following 30 years, in the absence of diplomatic relations, there was zero shipping between the two countries. A Chinese ship calling at a U.S. port, for instance, could have been seized by any American individual or company that claimed any of the assets frozen in China.

It was in the destiny of Stanley Barer to break this impasse.

---

31. Richard W. Larson, "Seattle Lawyer helped ship dock," *The Seattle Times*, Apr. 19, 1979, p. A14
32. Richard Halloran, "U.S. and China Open Ports to 2-Way Trade Under Private Accord," *The New York Times*, Feb. 24, 1979, p. 1

By 1975, Barer had left Washington, D.C. and joined the law firm Houger, Garvey & Schubert back in Seattle. His firm represented a number of clients including American importers of Chinese fireworks, a big commodity in those days, and a shipping company named Lykes Brothers Steamship Co. of New Orleans. Lykes needed to settle a long-standing damage claim involving one of its ships and a Chinese fishing vessel back in the early 1960s.

The legal work took Barer to China for the first time in 1975. He went there first to explain to the Chinese how to comply with U.S. labeling requirements for imported fireworks and then to negotiate with China Ocean Shipping Company (Cosco) a solution to the old claim.

With the relatively easy tasks done, Barer told the Chinese of Lykes' interest in resuming services to China and discussed with them the possibility of reciprocal shipping. When could Lykes' vessels call at Chinese ports? Barer asked. The Chinese replied, "When we can send our ships to America, your ships can call on China."[33]

Both Barer and the Chinese were well aware, of course, of the roadblock—the frozen assets problem. Trade between U.S. and China had in fact resumed in 1973 after each set up a liaison office in the other's country. But goods had to be carried by ships of third countries. The Chinese were anxious to put their own ships in American waters, but they couldn't because of the frozen-assets issue. They told Barer if he could find a way to circumvent the problem for Chinese ships, they would be ready to receive American ones. That was 1975. Normalization was still four years away.

Upon returning home, Barer took up his mission to find a way through the roadblock. He thought at first about proposing special legislation that would exempt foreign ships and planes from seizure to settle claims. Then he noticed an obscure piece of legislation called the Foreign Sovereign Immunities Act pending in the Congress. Although it was intended to bring legal procedures of the United States into line with those of other countries, Barer believed that one of the provisos would exempt certain kinds of foreign vessels from attachment in satisfaction of frozen assets claims. He waited and watched patiently while the bill moved

---

33. Bill DiBenedetto, "China: the mouse that roared," *Gulf Shipper*, May 3, 2004, link: http://www.gulfshipper.com/news/article.asp?ltype=feature&sid=426

slowly through Congress. As he had told himself, he would not contact the Chinese again until he found a way around the problem.

In October 1976, the Foreign Sovereign Immunities Act became law. Barer immediately prepared a legal brief contending that Chinese vessels could no longer be seized. He presented it first to long-time friend and fellow Seattleite, Transportation Secretary Adams. Then during the months that followed, Barer went about securing support from various government agencies. With Adams' help, Barer got support from the Carter White House, then Secretary of State Cyrus Vance, and most importantly then Attorney General Griffin Bell, who upheld Barer's opinion as valid.

In October 1978, Barer was ready. He and the President of Lykes, Mr. W. J. Amoss, Jr., took their legal case to Mr. Chai Zemin, then head of the Chinese liaison office in Washington, D.C., who would send it to Beijing. The Chinese reply came in December, inviting Barer and his client to Beijing in February. An agreement to resume direct bilateral shipping, as Barer pointed out in April 1979, had been essentially reached between private parties before President Carter's announcement on December 15, 1978 that the United States would give diplomatic recognition to China.[34]

On February 6, 1979, while Deng Xiaoping was flying home to Beijing via Japan after his visit to Seattle, Barer and his client were flying there, too, to finalize the "Lykes-Cosco Service Agreement". They had with them supporting letters from Sens. Magnuson and Jackson of Washington, Sen. Russell B. Long, Democrat of Louisiana, and Robert J. Blackwell, Assistant Secretary of Commerce for maritime affairs.

Four days later, on February 10, the first trade agreement on shipping lanes between China and the U.S. in 30 years was signed. The normalization of U.S. and China diplomatic relations in January and the settlement of frozen asset claims reached by the Chinese government and U.S. Treasury Secretary W. Michael Blumenthal in March had no effect on their agreement. As it was stated in the first paragraph of the agreement,

---

34.   Richard W. Larsen, "Seattle lawyer helped ship dock," *The Seattle Times*, Apr. 19, 1979, p. A14

"...The shipping service would begin 'now, before the signing of any maritime agreement between the government of the People's Republic of China and the United States of America and the settlement of problems of frozen assets held by' the two nations." [35]

One person as happy as Barer over the agreement was Sen. Magnuson, Barer's former boss and mentor. "Puget Sound's promise as the gateway to China is now beginning to be realized," [36] he claimed to the press.

Under this historic agreement, the first part of the deal was for the Letitia Lykes, a Lykes Brothers freighter, to arrive in Shanghai March 18. It did, amid cymbals, drums, flowers and free flowing mao tai, the Chinese national liquor. The Liu Lin Hai, under the second part of the agreement, was to dock in Seattle 30 days later. It did so, precisely.

But what exactly was the loophole that Barer saw in the Foreign Sovereign Immunities Act and how exactly did he argue his client's case? For that and many other questions, I visited Barer on a rare sunny winter afternoon in his office on Lake Union in Seattle. It was on the second floor, with a huge window looking out onto the shimmering water and white boats. Now chairman of a large holding company in the marine transportation industry and a regent of the University of Washington, his alma mater, Mr. Barer was warm and smiling. My mind worked quickly imagining how he must have smiled towards the Chinese crew coming down the gangplank of the Liu Lin Hai on that April day in 1979. When I showed him a newspaper clipping from 1979 with his photo in it, Barer said he had more hair then. I said he still had lots of hair. He did.

It was the first time I met and talked to Barer. But I had seen him once at the 25th anniversary gala of the Council. He left me with a deep impression. American Ambassador to China Mr. Clark Randt was giving a formal speech to the gathering. After praising the progress China had made in 25 years, Mr. Randt criticized China's human rights practice. When Mr. Randt was ready for questions, Barer was the first to stand up. He disagreed with the Ambassador's human rights comments. He said in effect that if we had to talk about China's

---

35.   Bill Prochnau, "China Shipping To Start in 'Month,'" *Seattle Post-Intelligencer*, Feb. 23, 1979, p. A1
36.   Ibid.

human rights, there was also Abu Ghraib. I remembered myself saying "Wow" quietly.

With that impression, I started asking Barer questions regarding the Liu Lin Hai as well as the beginning of the Council. Barer not only answered those questions, he also showed me the photos on the wall of him and Cosco officials in 1979 and gave me a copy of his collection of newspaper clippings on the Liu Lin Hai. By the end of the interview, I had learned not only about Barer's family trip to China, including a boat tour of the Three Gorges before the new dam construction, but also his take on China now, even on the redress of Tiananmen.

I did not forget to mention his questioning of Ambassador Randt's comment on China's human rights on that Council banquet night. Barer just said matter-of-factly, it was a time to celebrate, not criticize. So there was a time to celebrate and a time to criticize? What a unique ability on the part of Barer, as it occurred to me, the ability to separate China's achievement and its shortcomings! Not many people could do that. I came away feeling strongly that Barer was a true friend of China's, just like his former boss Sen. Magnuson.

With that meeting and follow-up emails, especially Barer's extra patience, I finally put together the most authoritative all-in-one account of the brilliant legal maneuvering that removed the roadblock in U.S. and China bilateral shipping. I am sure Barer tried hard to make it easier for me to understand:

> According to the law (the Foreign Sovereign Immunities Act), ships and aircraft of a socialist nation, as government property, used in official state business, while normally immune from claims by reason of sovereign immunity, would not be immune from frozen asset claims arising from seizure of private assets by the government. The converse of that must also be true. That is that the ships and aircraft of a socialist nation could have immunity from frozen asset claims if they were not engaged in official state business.

There must have been thousands of attorneys around the United States practicing in international business and/or representing clients in maritime transportation, and thousands of beautiful faces, too. It took one special attorney to launch the Liu Lin Hai and make history. It was Stanley H. Barer.

Barer said once of Sen. Magnuson, his mentor, "His conviction about peaceful trade with China had quite an impact on me. He made me look up and dream."[37]

That impact not only propelled Barer to launch the Liu Lin Hai's famous voyage, it was also to drive him to launch the Washington State China Relations Council. He was to play the "instrumental role" and give the "primary thrust" in founding the Council, as described by fellow founders. In a few years, Barer would also serve as the president of the Council.

"Celebrating the successful arrival of the Liu Lin Hai
on its maiden voyage to the U.S."
(Courtesy of Port of Seattle)

37. Richard W. Larsen, "Seattle lawyer helped ship dock," *The Seattle Times*, Apr. 19, 1979, p. A14

Stanley H. Barer, 2004

1.4

Dixy Lee Ray—Olympia's First China Trade Promoter—and Her Right-Hand Man Robert Anderson

Governor Dixy Lee Ray
(Courtesy of Washington State Archives.)

Robert C. Anderson, around 1979

Mr. Robert C. Anderson was appointed director of the Washington State Department of Commerce and Economic Development in early 1979. The department today is called the Washington State Department of Community, Trade & Economic Development.

As the director of the economic development agency, Anderson was in charge of the work of attracting, retaining, and expanding business in Washington state, assisting Washington businesses in the global marketplace, building international trade relationships, and advocating the importance of international trade to the state's economy.

Washington state had long been trading with European countries such as Great Britain and Germany, as well as with Latin America, Australia, and Japan. But except for Boeing's sales of 707s to China that began in 1972, the same year Nixon visited, there was nothing else going on between Washington state and China until the U.S.-China normalization in January of 1979 and Deng's visit in Seattle the following month. The new relations added a new item in Anderson's job description—building trade relations with China. As Mr. Anderson said, he was in the right place at right time.

He really was. But Anderson could not talk about the Washington state-China relations or the Council without talking about another "right", the right boss—Dixy Lee Ray, the governor—especially his trip to China with the governor in 1979 as her cabinet member.

I had read about that trip. It took place in the fall of 1979. But what was most unusual about the trip, as Anderson told me, was that Gov. Ray went to China at the personal invitation of none other than Vice Premier Deng Xiaoping. How did that happen? What did Gov. Ray do in China? Did the visit have anything to do with the founding of the Washington State China Relations Council?

For someone like me not familiar with Governor Dixy Lee Ray, it was truly an eye-opening experience to learn while searching for answers to the above questions.

Gov. Ray was the first woman governor of Washington state. Elected on November 3, 1976, she served from 1977 to 1981. Not only that. She had also been the first woman chair of the Atomic Energy Commission, the predecessor of the Department of Energy. Appointed to the post by President Nixon in 1972, she served in Washington D.C. from 1973 to 75.

But before she was the chairwoman of a federal agency and then governor of Washington state, Dixy Lee Ray was Dr. Ray, a renowned marine biologist who began teaching at the Zoology Department at the University of Washington in the mid 1940s. In 1963, she was appointed the director of the then new Seattle Pacific Science Center which had been part of the Seattle World's Fair of 1962.

It is known that the term "China Syndrome"—the description of an accidental nuclear reactor core meltdown with the fuel material sinking into the earth—was coined by the staff of the Atomic Energy Commission. As the head of the Commission, Gov. Ray was also known to have advocated the development of nuclear energy and educated the public about the safety issues. But when did Gov. Ray become interested in China?

As Anderson mentioned, Gov. Ray had been a favorite of President Nixon's. So some of Nixon's China enthusiasm must have been rubbed off on her. But there was more.

As it turned out, Gov. Ray was also someone who believed in free trade early on and understood the importance of international trade to the world economy, and especially to Washington state.

At an international trade conference held in May 1978 in Seattle, Gov. Ray talked about the international economic instability and protectionist trend in the world since the oil crisis in the early 1970s:

> "Many countries are now considering protectionist policies. They are gambling that their protectionist gains will not be offset by retaliatory action against their exports. They are ignoring the fact that if each country acts out of self-interest, the health of the entire world economy will suffer."[38]

She went on about how Washington state's economy depended on foreign trade to a much greater extent than most other states, and then said:

> "…if current events lead to a reduction of world trade through protectionism, recession or any other reason, we in the State of Washington have a great deal more to lose than most other states. For this reason, I believe it is in our best interest to explore the issues and seek ways to enhance rather than inhibit trade among nations."[39]

At the time, Washington state was already trading with Japan, South Korea, and Taiwan in Asia. Gov. Ray announced more steps that her administration was taking to assure the growth of Washington state's trade activities, among them:

- Opening of the State's first overseas representative office in Singapore to develop Southeast Asian trade opportunities;
- Arranging for a Japanese business consultant to act on behalf of the State of Washington in directing potential Japanese business investment to the state;

---

38. Dixy Lee Ray, "The Importance of Trade & An Open Policy of Washington State," *Washington State Archives,* for the Fourth Annual International Conference, May 18, 1978.
39. Ibid.

- Planning and promoting of the participation by Washington companies in overseas trade fairs and missions;
- Supporting and conducting export seminars for novice Washington exporters on the basic procedures of exporting and the business customs of major trading partners;
- Being involved in cultural exchanges between groups organized in Washington state and our friends all over the world.[40]

It was thus natural that when the United States and China normalized relations in 1979, Gov. Ray was ready for new opportunities between Washington state and China. It was natural that Gov. Ray warmly welcomed Deng Xiaoping to Seattle. It was also natural that Deng was so impressed with Ray's achievement as a scientist, a Nixon administration official as well as the governor of Washington state—home of the two China-friendly senators, advanced aircraft manufacturing, port facilities, and forest products—that he invited Gov. Ray to China. It was reported that Deng extended the invitation to her at the Washington Plaza luncheon on Feb. 4. It was the first such personal invitation from Deng Xiaoping to a governor rather than a head of state of a foreign country. And Gov. Ray accepted it on the spot.

On Sept. 15, 1979, Gov. Ray boarded a Japan Airlines plane from Vancouver, B.C., for China on a weeklong visit. On her delegation were, of course, Mr. Anderson, along with Taul Watanabe, Vice President of the Burlington Northern Railroad in Seattle, a friend and one of the governor's economic advisors; Bruce McPhaden, Vice President of Kaiser Aluminum Co., Spokane, and a close confidant of the governor; Fred Tolan, a trucking consultant from Seattle; William Franklin, Vice President of Weyerhaeuser Co., Federal Way; two Washington State security personnel, William Keller and Vernon Griffith; and two members of KOMO-TV, reporter Ruth Walsh and cameraman Mahlon Brosseau. Mrs. Marion Reid, Governor Ray's sister and official hostess at the executive mansion, was on the trip, too.

Before departure, Gov. Ray said,

> "It is a business-oriented trip, to find a market for some of Washington state's products and probably more immediately to encourage the use of our ports, particularly the Port of Seattle, for the two-way trade of the ships that will be

---

40. Ibid.

coming bearing the goods that China is expecting to put on the market in this country." [41]

It was indeed a business trip. As Anderson also remembered, during their stay in Beijing, members of the delegation visited the Chinese ministries of forestry, metallurgical industry, railways and the bureau of oceanography. The most important of their meetings was, of course, with Vice Premier Deng Xiaoping in the Great Hall of the People.

But before the meeting became serious, Anderson told me, the delegation got to see up close the humorous side of Deng.

Gov. Ray was well known in Olympia for her strong distaste for cigarette smoke or cigarette smokers. Staff would refrain from smoking in the same building with her. But that day, Deng, as a chain smoker, lit up right away and began puffing and blowing in Ray's direction. Ray was very uncomfortable until she heard what Deng was saying, "…I understand in some countries people are denied basic freedoms…people who smoke are isolated in special rooms…"[42] she began to laugh.

Mr. Anderson laughed, too, re-telling me the episode.

Gov. Ray and the delegation discussed with Deng the opening up of trade between Washington state and China. As she told reporters, Deng was very interested in the three areas she presented—namely forestry development and use of forestry products, mining and milling of light minerals, railroad development and the movement of freight—and even suggested that there should be specific programs developed from the visit.[43]

Gov. Ray also related how Deng regarded Seattle with great affection and spoke at some length about the warm hospitality he had received.

---

41. Mike Layton, "Dixy Taking Off On Far East Trade Trip," *Seattle Post-Intelligencer*, Sept. 15, 1979.

42. William Franklin, retired president of Weyerhaeuser Asia, "A China Policy Built on Realism, Respect," *The Seattle Times*, August 7, 1997, op-ed.

43. "Ray's welcome warm at Chinese trade talk," *The Spokesman Review*, Sept. 21, 1979

A few days after her return to Seattle, Gov. Ray, along with Mr. Anderson, gave a special news conference on the trip—the first governor's trade mission to China of Washington state, or any state.

Filled with confidence and hope for the new opportunities, Gov. Ray said, "I believe that as a result of our visit…the ties of communications and understanding are being developed between our state and China, and that this will lead to a lot of activity in the future and that down the line we should expect increased trade and eventually economic benefits."[44]

China wouldn't be a market for "widgets" for years, she pointed out, but Chinese officials had shown strong interest in reforestation, development of mineral deposits, and establishing a modern transportation system. That's why, she concluded, "I believe that among the first things that will happen will be technical missions, exchanges of people, both coming from China to our state and from our state to China, to assist in the kind of planning and early stages of development of these areas."[45]

Well on target! By the time Gov. Ray gave that news conference, the Washington State China Relations Council had already been incorporated. It was precisely in the expectation of those missions and exchanges to come and with the purpose of promoting and facilitating them that the Council was created. And it was created just in time. Governor Ray knew what she was talking about. So did Anderson.

As a matter of fact, Anderson told me, during the spring of that year, after Deng Xiaoping had gone home from Seattle and with the realization of how important trade with China was becoming to Washington state, Anderson and Gov. Ray discussed what to do politically and economically. It seemed appropriate, Anderson said, that a non-profit and private organization be formed, a council, initiated from his office and the governor's office, which would be directly involved in dealing with China.

---

44. Lyle Burt, "Ray: Technical experts may be sent to China," *The Seattle Times*, Oct. 2, 1979, p. A8
45. Ibid.

By the fall of 1979, the Council was not only formed, Anderson was also serv-ing as its first president. Neither would have been possible without Gov. Ray's personal attention and endorsement.

As for Anderson's new responsibilities at the Council, Gov. Ray said to her right-hand man that it was O.K., "As long as you do the rest of your work."

Washington State trade delegation to China, September 1979.
Vice Premier Deng is in the middle, 1st row; Gov. Ray is on his left.
Anderson is on the far right.
(Washington State China Relations Council archives.)

Robert C. Anderson, 2005

1.5

The Closest Port to China and Its Young Director James Dwyer

James D. Dwyer, 1979

After returning from Beijing with the Lykes-Cosco contract and before Liu Lin Hai came over, Stanley Barer also sought help from a friend at the Port of Seattle, James D. Dwyer, another of the Council founders, also the youngest.

Readers may remember the tour of the Port of Seattle by the Chinese delegation in February 1979. But readers may not know that it was the Chinese that had requested the tour, as well as the one of Boeing. In fact, it was Deng Xiaoping who had first expressed an interest in Seattle's port facilities, as revealed by

Sen. Henry Jackson after a visit to Beijing earlier that year.[46] The Chinese knew that the Port of Seattle was one the most modern in the world.

Not just known for its facilities, the Port of Seattle was also known to offer the closest route between the U.S. and China, 15 hours closer to the main Chinese port of Shanghai than Oakland or San Francisco, 30 hours closer than Long Beach or Los Angeles. This was very important, as Dwyer said in March 1979, because "those ships are extremely expensive to operate—between $30,000 and $50,000 a day, so your sailing time and your time in the harbor are very critical."[47]

When Sen. Magnuson had mentioned this sailing advantage at the 600-person luncheon for Deng Xiaoping in February, it had brought the house down. It also had brought protest from a visitor from Honolulu who shouted, "The closest U.S. port to China isn't Seattle...it's not on West Coast. It's in Hawaii."[48]

But the protest was in vain. For it was not only the sailing distance, there were also a number of other factors which included the history of trade between the Port of Seattle and China beginning in lumber and tung oil exchanges in the mid–1800s, the presence nearby of The Boeing Co. that had already sold almost $300 million of commercial jets and parts to the Chinese since Nixon's visit, good rail and truck distribution lines to other markets of the U.S., Eastern Washington's "soft wheat," and the $100 million of new port facilities, etc.,[49] that altogether made the Port of Seattle No. 1 on China's port list for a first ship call.

It was at this port that James D. Dwyer, at age of 32, was already the No. 2 person in 1979, as its Senior Director for Port Development and Relations.

Barer stopped Dwyer at a party one day and asked if he could bring the first vessel from the People's Republic of China into the United States, to Seattle,

---

46. George Foster, "China, Northwest Clasp Hands," *Seattle Post-Intelligencer*, Feb. 3, 1979, p. A1
47. William Trombley, "Seattle Puts Out Welcome Mat for China," *LA Times*, Mar. 12, 1979, p.2
48. Shelby Scates, "Pragmatic Chinese, Practical Seattle," *Seattle Post-Intelligencer*, Feb. 5, 1979, p. A3
49. William Trombley, "Seattle Puts Out Welcome Mat for China," *LA Times*, Mar. 12, 1979, p. 12

could the Port guarantee him docking, berth, stevedoring, and security? Dwyer answered yes, without a moment's hesitation.

Dwyer had just been given a new line of work at the port: China business development. Not only was he learning everything he could about China since Deng Xiaoping's visit in February, he was also planning his own first China adventure in May. After the conversation between the two, Dwyer worked closely with Barer for the coming visit of the Liu Lin Hai. The result was on all the smiling faces at Pier 91 that day, Chinese and American.

But there was more than festivity on Dwyer's mind. The welcoming ceremony for the Liu Lin Hai came and went, a new future, however, had just begun for the Port of Seattle and China.

For the occasion of the Liu Lin Hai's arrival, China had sent a delegation of shipping officials including Mr. Peng Deqing, Vice Minister of Communications, the Ministry in charge of China's shipping, and Mr. Zheng Zhongyuan, Deputy General Manager of China Ocean Shipping Company, or Cosco.[50] For Dwyer and his colleagues, it was an opportunity to play good host and make new friends.

And they did. They took the Chinese delegation and the Liu Lin Hai crew on a tour of Elliott Bay in a boat named Goodtime III, showing them the Port of Seattle facilities. They then treated the visitors to a banquet of prime rib and baked Alaska at the Washington Plaza Hotel.[51] But Dwyer did more. He took the whole crew of the Liu Lin Hai to his home. That was more than 40 people!

But before the Chinese shipping delegation left for a tour of five other U.S. ports including Oakland, San Francisco, Galveston, Houston and New Orleans, Dwyer and Henry L. Kotkins, President of Port of Seattle Commission, discussed with Vice Minister Peng the idea of establishing a "sister" port relationship between the Port of Seattle and a appropriate port in China. There was not much time, but they had started an important dialogue.

---

50. Joe Frisno, "The First Chinese Flagship in 30 Years Arrives Today," *Seattle Post-Intelligencer*, Apr. 18, 1979, p. A1
51. Bill Prochnau, "Symbolic Reunion As a Chinese Ship Docks Here," *Seattle Post-Intelligencer*, Apr. 19, 1979, p. A1

Later that April, Dwyer and Kotkins followed up the conversation with the Chinese with a letter campaign. Joining them were Sen. Magnuson, Sen. Jackson, Seattle Mayor Charles Royer, King County Executive John Spellman, and Gov. Ray. These state, county and city leaders either wrote or endorsed letters to the Chinese officials such as Mr. Chai Zemin, the Chinese Ambassador, Mr. Zeng Shang, Minister of Communications, and Mr. Chai Pao-Chan, Director of Bureau of Ports and Harbors.

The enthusiasm for friendly relations with a Chinese port was perhaps best expressed by Sen. Magnuson in his letter to Minister Zeng dated April 27, 1979:

> "The docking in Seattle of the 'Liu Lin Hai' carried special significance for me since it marked the start of shipping between our countries, a goal toward which I have worked for many, many years…I am also happy to join with Senator Jackson, the Governor, the President of the Port of Seattle Commission, the Mayor of Seattle, and the King County Executive in urging that the Port of Seattle and one of your great ports enter into a 'sister port' relationship."[52]

But one Chinese port that Dwyer and Seattle's leaders preferred was the Port of Shanghai, as shown clearly in the letter addressed to Minister Zeng by Henry Kotkins and Mayor Royer that Dwyer attached in his letter to Director Chai of Bureau of Ports and Harbors:

> "For as long as Seattle has been an operating port, it has enjoyed trade with Shanghai. Dating back to the early 1920s Seattle has received 25% of all Chinese exports to the U.S., the bulk of that amount coming from Shanghai. Furthermore, Shanghai is a city that has meant a great deal personally to the honorable U.S. Senators from the State of Washington, Senator Warren Magnuson and Senator Henry Jackson. Both have spent a considerable amount of time in Shanghai and both men have very fond memories and feelings about that city."[53]

With all the letters sent and with April turning into May, Dwyer was ready to go to China. Eager to hear him tell his first China adventure, I visited Dwyer in his Northgate office, a black glass tower.

Dwyer, now President and CEO of the Washington Dental Service, was easygoing and ready to laugh. After leaving the Port of Seattle in the late 1980s as its

---

52. Port of Seattle archives on Liu Lin Hai.
53. Ibid.

executive director after 16 years of service, Dwyer had held a number of executive positions in law and in business.

Sitting across a coffee table, Dwyer started to recall the trip 25 years earlier.

It was on May 4, 1979, Dwyer arrived in Beijing with 24 other executives of industry, agriculture, technology, research and services in the Seattle area. The mission, a first, was organized by the Washington Council on International Trade, or WCIT. As a private association, WCIT was set up in 1973 with the leadership of Dr. George Taylor, a renowned Asia scholar and a community leader. Dr. Taylor was also credited with the creation of the Far Eastern and Russian Institute at the University of Washington, the predecessor of the Jackson School of International Studies. Of course, Sens. Jackson and Magnuson had helped arrange for the mission.

The person who sent Dwyer on this trip was Richard D. Ford, then Port of Seattle executive director. It was also Ford that had given Dwyer the assignment of developing China business. And earlier, Ford had also helped found WCIT. In Deng Xiaoping's visit as well as the Liu Lin Hai's docking, Mr. Ford saw great potential in store for the Port of Seattle in the newly normalized relations with China. Good at delegating and using young talent, Ford told Dwyer that now his task was to go to China.

So Dwyer did, along with Henry Kotkins and Merle Adlum, another Port of Seattle Commissioner. Armed with a draft proposal for sister-port relations between Seattle and Shanghai, Dwyer's task was no laughing matter. But he laughed when he described to me how he had stayed in the only hotel for foreigners at the time, the Beijing Hotel, and tried for four days to find the office of Cosco. It turned out that it was right across the street from the hotel!

Dwyer of course didn't waste all four days just looking for Cosco's office. He met again with Vice Minister Peng, who, having just returned to Beijing from the tour of U.S. ports, took Dwyer and the group to a famous Peking duck restaurant. Dwyer discussed further with Peng the sister-port relationship and presented Peng the draft proposal. Before leaving Beijing, Dwyer, of course, finally found and met again with Mr. Zheng, Deputy General Manager of Cosco, who had been in Seattle for the Liu Lin Hai.

Next, it was on to Shanghai, the "sister" that the Port of Seattle had in mind. Dwyer and the two colleagues had the opportunity of meeting and discussing the sister-port relationship with Mr. Li Chishan, Director of Shanghai Port, and other Shanghai officials. Dwyer left them with a copy of the proposal, too.

Dwyer got to relax a little after that as the delegation toured Hangzhou, Suzhou, and then Guangzhou.

Once back in Seattle, however, there was no more relaxing. Following up on the positive response from the Chinese on the concept of the sister-port relationship, Dwyer started writing letters again in early June. He sent the Chinese a modified copy of the proposed agreement. He updated Sens. Magnuson, Jackson and Mayor Royer on the matter. He discussed with the Chinese about sending a Port of Seattle technical delegation to China in September and a return visit by the Chinese to Seattle in early 1980. He expressed his hope that the agreement between Ports of Seattle and Shanghai could be signed in September during the visit of the Port of Seattle delegation.

For someone who had just taken on the new task of developing China business, Dwyer performed the job with flying colors.

In late September of 1979, while Dwyer was attending a senior business management program at Harvard, Mr. Ford led a five-member technical delegation from the Port of Seattle to China as the guest of the Ministry of Communications. They gave seminars in various Chinese ports, providing information on port development. But the seminars were only the prelude to what was to come in Shanghai.

On September 25, the agreement Dwyer worked so hard for, "Agreement Between the Port of Seattle of the United States and the Port of Shanghai of the People's Republic of China for Establishing Friendship-Port Relationship," was signed. Mr. Richard Ford, representing the Port of Seattle, and Mr. Li Chishan, representing the Port of Shanghai, were the signatories. It was the first such agreement between ports of the United States and China since normalization, and the first such arrangement in the world for Shanghai.

Pleased was an understatement for Dwyer upon learning the news. But he couldn't make it to Shanghai from Harvard. He didn't even make it back to Seattle in time for the birth of his first child, a son, in December that year. He was two hours late.

But Dwyer didn't wait to get busy again, receiving the first Cosco delegation in February 1980, planning the return visit of the Shanghai delegation for June, and arranging for the three-month internship in Seattle of four Port of Shanghai engineers later that year. He proved himself worthy of the charge Mr. Ford had given him: China business development.

I wondered aloud, before leaving Dwyer's office, if he was not doing anything with China now. He said he was. As the chairman of the board of the Seattle Organizing Committee, he was helping to organize, in partnership with the U.S. Olympic Committee, the Pacific Rim Sports Summit to be held in the Seattle area in summer of 2005. They had started out with the concept of a US-China sports summit but expanded it to the Pacific Rim to meet the wider response in the region.

So, Dwyer was just onto something bigger.

James D. Dwyer, 2005

1.6

Femme Internationale—Our UN Alumna Patricia Baillargeon

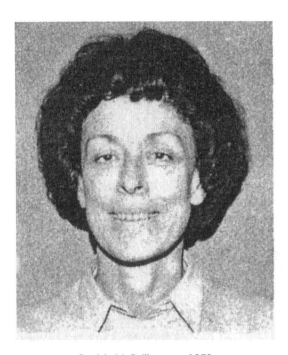

Patricia M. Baillargeon, 1979

Of the five people who incorporated the Washington State China Relations Council, there was only one woman. She had to be special, and she is. Her name is Patricia M. Baillargeon.

One does not meet often someone who once worked for Eleanor Roosevelt and the United Nations. But Ms. Baillargeon is one, and she assisted Mrs. Roosevelt with her UN work for seven years, 1953 to 1960. It takes on more meaning to get to know someone like Baillargeon this year, 2005, the 60th anniversary of the UN.

One also does not meet often someone with a well-known family. Baillargeon is one, too. Most probably recognize her last name, the name of the Baillargeon family of Seattle, a name that is in Who's Who in Washington and the History of King County.

The Baillargeons were originally from France, emigrating to Canada. The family moved to the United States in 1867.[54]Ms. Baillargeon's grandfather went on to become a successful merchant in Seattle, known as the proprietor of The Lace House, a fine dry goods store once located in the Collins Building at the southeast corner of Second Avenue and James Street. The building, restored in 2001, is still standing today.[55]

Baillargeon's father Cebert Baillargeon, born in Seattle in 1889, served in the United States Navy during World War I and on the United States Commission to Negotiate Peace in Paris in 1918–19.[56]Until his death in 1964, he was chairman and CEO of Seattle Trust & Savings Bank,[57]a mid-sized bank bought in 1987 by Key Bank. Mr. Baillargeon had been a leading businessman, philanthropist, and civic leader. His long list of titles included past presidency to a variety of organizations such as the Seattle Chamber of Commerce, Seattle Symphony Orchestra and Seattle China Club.[58]

Seattle China Club! Around the time I started working on this book, I attended a dinner organized by the Seattle China Club. I was amazed to learn that the Club had been set up as early as 1916. Its brochure read:

> The mission of the China Club of Seattle is to increase the awareness, understanding and appreciation of developments in Chinese culture, history, philosophy, and current affairs. We believe it is important to enhance the means for social and commercial interchange between our respective cultures.

---

54. Rev. H.K. Hines, D. D., An Illustrated History of the State of Washington, The Lewis Publishing Co., Chicago, IL 1893, http://freepages.genealogy.rootsweb.com/~jtenlen/jabaillargeon.txt
55. Paul Dorpat, "An Artful Restoration," *The Seattle Times: Pacific Northwest Magazine,* http://seattletimes.nwsource.com/pacificnw/2003/0126/nowthen.html
56. C.B. Bagley, *History of King County Washington* (Chicago-Seattle: The S. J. Clarke Publishing Company, 1929) p. 420
57. The Seattle Times, Dec. 25, 1964
58. Hugh L. White, *Who's Who in Washington*, 1962, p. 190–191

That was some special club! Even if the China in the name of the club had gone through various governments from that of Sun Yat-sen to Chiang Kai-shek to Mao Zedong to Deng Xiaoping, the club has never changed its mission.

For Baillargeon, two questions looming large in my head were: How did a girl from a business family in Seattle get to work in New York for perhaps the most admired First Lady of the country? How did she then team up with four men back in Seattle in founding a council on China?

Baillargeon met me at the Council at 4 p.m. on a Friday. I had never met her. She was not tall but was sharp, dress-wise and speech-wise, after all these years, even on a Friday afternoon. I asked her how come she did not join the family business and instead had a totally different career.

It turned out that young Patricia had something else in mind early on. For college, she went to one of the nation's top women's schools: Mills College, in California. She earned a B.A. in history and government. That was their political science, she told me. But before Mills, she had also gone to a two-year college in Boston, far from home. That combination of East Coast exposure and political science had prepared Baillargeon well for the launch of her unique career.

As the longest serving and until then the most active First Lady of the United States, Mrs. Roosevelt said in her sorrow over the death of President Roosevelt in 1945, "The story is over."[59]But it was not. That year, not only did she become a board member of the NAACP, she was also appointed by President Harry Truman to the United States delegation to the United Nations. Elected chair of the UN Human Rights Commission in 1947, she spearheaded the work of drafting the Universal Declaration of Human Rights and saw to its adoption by the UN General Assembly in December 1948. She continued serving on the commission until 1952.

The following year, Mrs. Roosevelt began volunteering her services to AAUN—the American Association for the United Nations—the predecessor of the United Nations Association of the United States of America (UNA-USA) of today. She needed an assistant.

---

59. Ann Mary, "A Timeline On Eleanor Roosevelt," http://pblmm.k12.ca.us/projects/ discrimination/Women/WomenThroughYears/aatl.html

Along came Baillargeon. Independent, motivated, and armed with a degree in political science, she volunteered at a UN conference in Washington D.C. With a previous job offer there frozen by the federal government, she asked about opportunities at the UN. She was offered the assistant position to Mrs. Roosevelt for six weeks. Two weeks later, she was hired to work for Mrs. Roosevelt permanently.

As an organization designed to inform the public about the work of the United Nations and to insure more effective American participation in the UN, AAUN could use all the services of Mrs. Roosevelt, who was reputed for her skills and friendliness in talking to ordinary people. Throughout the mid and late-1950s, Mrs. Roosevelt traveled throughout the country, from big cities to small towns to college campuses, speaking to various groups in an effort to bring about understanding and support for the UN.

As Mrs. Roosevelt's assistant, Baillargeon was not only on all those tours, she helped organize them. They traveled to all 50 states, some more than once. Baillargeon also traveled to Asia and Europe for the AAUN.

At the AAUN office, Mrs. Roosevelt received thousands of letters, invitations, requests and inquiries. It fell upon Baillargeon to draft the reply letters. She also researched for a book Mrs. Roosevelt wrote on the UN.

Working for Mrs. Roosevelt day in and day out all those years, with their desks facing each other, Baillargeon had learned a great deal from Mrs. Roosevelt, as a woman, an activist, an internationalist, and a human rights champion.

So much so that after returning to Seattle, Baillargeon told me, she worked for the Open Housing campaign for six months. It was in 1963, the same year Dr. Martin Luther King made his "I Have A Dream" speech. She said, after all that work for the UN and with foreign delegates, she couldn't believe the discrimination in housing sales and rentals in Seattle.

It was indeed unbelievable. On July 1st, 1963, over 400 people rallied at Seattle City Hall to protest delays in passing an open-housing law.[60] About two weeks

---

60. HistoryLink, "Seattle votes down open housing on March 10, 1964," http://www.washington.historylink.org/output.cfm?file_id=3154

later, after the city formed a 12-member Human Rights Commission with only two blacks on it, a sit-in at City Hall followed. It was there that Seattle saw its first civil-rights arrests.[61]That October, Baillargeon marched with scores of others from the Space Needle to downtown in support of the Open Housing campaign.

The open housing law, which banned racial restrictions in private housing, was not passed by the City Council until 1968.[62]Three years before that, in 1965, Baillargeon was one of two finalists for appointment to fill vacancy on the Seattle City Council, following the untimely death of Council member Wing Luke, who had advocated for an open housing law. In 1967, Baillargeon was also one of the founding board members of the Wing Luke Asian Museum.

But open housing campaign was not all in which Baillargeon was involved. She also worked at the Seattle World's Fair in 1962, the fair that put Seattle on the world's map. As assistant protocol officer, she coordinated the 23 official exhibitor countries from Europe and Asia. She worked for two years there, before and after the six-month exhibition.

As if Baillargeon did not already have enough international experience, she went to work next for the Consulate General of Japan, from 1963 to 67. As the assistant to the consul general, she worked on correspondence, wrote speeches, issued news releases and conducted research on American trade legislation affecting Japan, especially that of trade protection.

It all seemed natural that after Baillargeon arrived to work at the Port of Seattle as its first woman executive in 1967, she was sent to Japan for two months to work at a trade fair. The office where Baillargeon worked first as an assistant director and then director (1973–75) was called the Department of World Trade Center. It had two lines of work: studying the possibility of building a world trade center along the waterfront and running the Washington State International Trade Fair (WSITF), or simply the Trade Fair, which was partially funded by the Port. Baillargeon started her tenure of directorship at a significant time, for the Trade Fair had just made the important transition from organizing import fairs to organizing export fairs for Washington state products.

---

61. The Seattle Times, "Martin Luther King, Jr.," http://seattletimes.nwsource.com/ mlk/king/timeline.html
62. HistoryLink, "Seattle votes down open housing on March 10, 1964," http:// www.washington.historylink.org/output.cfm?file_id=3154

While still the director of the World Trade Center Department, Baillargeon was asked by Mr. Richard Ford, that same boss of James Dwyer's, to help organize the Washington Council on International Trade (WCIT.) She gladly did. Not only did she know Dr. Taylor, she had done a foreign studies survey for him at the University of Washington School of International Studies right after her return to Seattle from New York. Several years later, as a WCIT executive committee member, Baillargeon was also to help Dr. Taylor plan WCIT's first mission to China.

When it comes to China, the major influence on Baillargeon must have come from Mrs. Roosevelt, who had a strong interest in China and had pushed for the return of the People's Republic to the UN.

Mrs. Roosevelt had long wanted to go to China. In 1957, as the author of the very popular syndicated column "My Day," Mrs. Roosevelt applied for a visa to visit China to interview Chinese leaders on behalf of one of the newspapers. She was told by the State Department, however, that no newsman was permitted by the U.S. government to visit Communist China.

That was when she wrote her famous June 25 column titled "I Was Denied a Visa to Red China." In it, Mrs. Roosevelt wrote,

> "I still hope that the State Department may find it possible to allow all correspondents who wish to gather news from this area of the world to go there if the Chinese will allow them to enter."[63]

> "The difficulties we face with any Communist country are still considerable, but I believe that trade and communication are essential if we are ever to come to some solution of how to live in the same world, in spite of our differences, without war."[64]

Trade and communication essential, with a Communist country, like China? Didn't that sound familiar? Didn't that remind one of Washington state's Maggie and Scoop?

---

63. The Eleanor Papers, The Human Rights Years, 1945–1962, http://www.gwu.edu/~erpapers/documents/columns/md19570625.html
64. Ibid.

After leaving the Port of Seattle, Baillargeon became an international trade consultant, a very successful one, too. She had her own office in downtown Seattle and a variety of clients, from trading companies to government agencies of other states. In 1977, she was even offered the post of Director of the Washington State Department of Commerce and Economic Development by Governor Dixy Lee Ray. However, she remained a consultant. In May 1979, it was in the capacity of a trade consultant that Baillargeon went on the WCIT China mission, representing a number of clients interested in import and export with China as well as the Washington State International Trade Fair.

The fact that Baillargeon was the only official female member on that WCIT mission as well as the only woman among the founders of the Council speaks volumes. With her rich and wide experience in international affairs and international trade, who wouldn't have wanted Baillargeon on board, especially for an organization like the Washington State China Relations Council? That she was female and a Baillargeon was irrelevant. The following list of some of the boards and committees Baillargeon has served on only makes her stand out more as a highly accomplished person:

> Seattle-Christchurch (N.Z.) Sister City Committee—founding board member;
> Seattle-Tashkent Sister City Committee—founding board member
> Seattle-Kobe Sister City Committee
> United Nations Association of the USA—National Board
> World Affairs Council—Board
> Seattle Chamber of Commerce—Word Trade Committee
> Northwest Regional China Council
> Asia Society—Northwest Council Board

I now understand why Baillargeon could only find time to meet me the first time on a late Friday afternoon. Today, Baillargeon is busy as ever. She consults. She gives speeches about her experience with Mrs. Roosevelt. She has also been preparing materials for a manuscript on her years with Mrs. Roosevelt. In fact, the first return I got Googling her was the schedule of her speech at the City Club of Tacoma. The topic: Eleanor Roosevelt—Legacy of Leadership.

When I commented once in a telephone conversation with Baillargeon that her work seemed to have become more trade oriented after her stint at the Japanese Consulate, she disputed that. She said she had always believed that trade was the link to everything. She then quoted to me the late Sen. Magnuson, "Trade is the tool of peace."

Who could dispute that or Baillargeon?

Patricia M. Baillargeon, 2005

1.7

Trading with a Former Enemy—Our Korean War Veteran Richard Kirk

Richard L. Kirk, 1993

Of the five founders of the Washington State China Relations Council, the one with most dramatic and unexpected career path had to be Mr. Richard L. Kirk.

When I started working on this book, Mr. Kirk had already been retired for quite some time. He had not been in touch with the Council much. Neither Mr. Borich nor the other founders I had interviewed knew Kirk's whereabouts or current contact information. I Googled him many times, but without luck. I was at a loss. How could I have a complete story of the Council without finding or finding out about one of its founders?

The all-knowing Ms. Baillargeon came to the rescue. I had actually just located her and mentioned to her that I was looking for Mr. Kirk. She told me that Kirk lived in Tacoma. Tacoma? What a clue! Now I had a specific geographical parameter to search.

I indeed found Kirk, or his whereabouts, immediately! In fact, I saw a news brief in The Sun newspaper of Bremerton online about his appointment in 1999 by Governor Locke to the State Veterans Affairs Advisory Committee.[65] The committee advised the governor and the director of the State Department of Veterans Affairs on the needs and concerns of veterans. I contacted the Department of Veterans Affairs. A couple of days later, a phone message was waiting for me when I got home. It was from Kirk!

Kirk and his wife did live in Tacoma. They had moved there from Seattle a number of years ago. They had come to like Tacoma so much that they now thought of Seattle as Tacoma's suburb.

Kirk and I met at the Allenmore public golf course next to his condo home. Yes, Kirk played golf there. Very gentlemanly and friendly, Kirk started chatting with me right in the parking lot. It was drizzling that morning. We went into the café on the site.

At the time we sat down and talked, Kirk had already served two three-year terms as the advisor to the governor on the state's veteran affairs. The 1999 appointment was in fact a reappointment. I was eager to find out what kind of veteran experience Kirk had that made Gov. Locke appoint him in the first place. I was not disappointed.

Mr. Kirk, or Lt. Col. Kirk, had served in the U.S. Army for 25 years. He had fought in WWII, in both Africa and Europe. He also served in Germany during the post-war occupation. But it was his experience in the Korean War, especially in the Battle at the Chosin, that defined Kirk's military career.

Chosin was the name of a reservoir in North Korea, near Northeast China, and was one of the farthest points of the allied advance toward China. It was

---

65. The Sun, http://web.kitsapsun.com/westsound99/roundup/99sept/0917ws.html, Sept. 17, 1999

there that China entered the war, surprised the allies and began pushing them back. The battle was fought for two weeks during November and December of 1950, in minus-30 degree temperatures. It pitted 15,000 allied forces, mostly American marines and infantry, against 120,000 Chinese infantrymen. Kirk was a member of the 3rd Infantry Division just south of the Reservoir charged with covering the withdrawal of the Marines from the Reservoir. When the battle was over, 3,000 of the allied forces had been killed and 6,000 wounded. On the Chinese side, there were 25,000 killed and 12,500 wounded.[66]

According to historians, the Battle at the Chosin was the most savage and bloodiest in modern warfare in terms of the ratio of casualties to Americans engaged. Time magazine described as "…. unparalleled in U. S. military history…an epic of great suffering and great valor."[67] It was exactly for that suffering and valor that Kirk and those who emerged from Chosin received a Presidential Unit Citation.[68] It was also the same suffering and valor that led Kirk and his fellow surviving comrades to form an eternal band of brothers called the Chosin Few. There were once 5,000 members of the Chosin Few across the country, with about 100 them in Washington state.[69] Kirk had served on the Board of the Few for four years.

Over a cup of coffee, with a moist golf course outside the window, and some seniors enjoying their get-together at other tables, Kirk recalled for me some of the scenes of the Chosin 55 years earlier—the frostbite cases in the 30-below temperatures, the very young, very brave but very poorly-equipped Chinese soldiers, and the two Chinese words for surrender he had been taught to say, etc. He even tried out the two words "tou xiang" on me. Luckily, Kirk never had to use them in Chosin.

I couldn't put the picture together. On one side was a young American soldier, fighting the Chinese in Korea in life-and-death battles in the 1950s. On the other was a mature gentleman, in the summer of 1979, signing the incorporation papers of a non-profit organization to promote relations with China! Yet, they were both Mr. Kirk.

---

66. The Chosin Few, "Purpose of The Few," http://home.hawaii.rr.com/chosin/
67. Ibid.
68. Ibid.
69. Alex Tizon, "Others may forget this war, but they cannot," *The Seattle Times*, Jun. 25, 2000

What happened in between? How did one become the other?

It turned out that Kirk was not just a courageous soldier, he was also a talented linguist. With two years of training in Japanese language during the war, Kirk was stationed with the Army in Korea from 1945–1948. For about two years, Kirk was in command of a translator team. His work involved having Korean translators translate Korean into Japanese first, selecting and translating Japanese headlines himself, and then having Nisei members of the team translate Japanese articles into English. But Japanese was not the only foreign language in which Kirk was fluent. He was also fluent in German, and with working knowledge of French and Spanish.

After retiring from the Army in 1967, Kirk, with his international experience, especially his Asian knowledge and language abilities, went on to work the following year as a foreign trade specialist at the Washington State Department of Commerce and Economic Development. It was the same department to which Mr. Robert Anderson would be appointed director in the late 1970s.

For the next eight years, Kirk concerned himself with matching Washington state industry and trade with foreign markets and helping companies sell goods and services to other countries. He familiarized himself with the industrial and agricultural products of the state and looked for markets for them. When he found markets, he would persuade the companies to participate in trade shows in the international marketplace. Kirk said that he had put emphasis on Washington State's relationship with countries in the Pacific Rim, although he and companies had participated in shows in Europe and Australia.

Kirk was a diligent and resourceful trade specialist. To arrange financing and credit verification and to get the products to the market with the best rates available, he worked with various organizations, including banks and financial institutions here and in foreign countries, offices and services of the federal government, the international offices of the Port of Seattle, and local freight forwarders and customs house brokers. During those years, Kirk was back in Asia a number of times, not as an army man, but as a leader of trade missions.

Now I could see the direction of Kirk's career change and the connection between Kirk the military officer and Kirk a founder of the Washington State

China Relations Council. But there was more—the Washington State International Trade Fair (WSITF).

The WSITF was the same Trade Fair that was part of Ms. Baillargeon's job at the Port of Seattle. As the oldest trade organization in Washington state, it was first set up in 1951 to facilitate trade between Washington state and Japan and later expanded to support other Pacific Northwest states in their efforts to increase trade with countries all over the world. The Trade Fair was once financially supported by the state government, especially Kirk's department, as well as by the Port of Seattle, especially Baillargeon's department.

Having used the name the International Trade and Exhibitor Services for some time, the Trade Fair today is again called the Washington State International Trade Fair. With a mission to support businesses to promote their products, services and brands, it organizes pavilions at a wide variety of trade shows in Asia, Europe and South America, representing target sectors for the whole Pacific Northwest region. But what does it have to do with Kirk?

After retiring from the State, Kirk became president of the WSITF in 1975. By then, the Trade Fair already had its own office. In that post, Kirk went on to work for almost another decade, till 1984. Some retiring that was. As Kirk told me, at the WSITF, he simply continued what he had been doing in the Department of Commerce and Economic Development, that is, to help Washington's industry and agriculture trade in foreign markets, such as Japan, Taiwan, and even the former Soviet Union—but of course, not China,

One could imagine what effect the normalization of diplomatic relations between U.S. and China in January 1979 had on the WSITF and the companies it represented. One could also imagine what Kirk felt attending the Deng luncheon at the Washington Plaza Hotel in February. It all seemed natural that Kirk was to join four others in August that year as one of the founders of the Council representing the WSITF, the oldest international trade organization in Washington state and one of the oldest of its kind in the country.

Kirk also realized the need for a China-focused organization because China was the next market, a market of a billion people. But he gives credit to others, especially to Stanley Barer, as the primary thrust in founding the Council.

Kirk, however, made his own mark soon after. As the executive director of the Washington State International Trade Fair, he had been exploring opportunities for Chinese trade show activity in Washington state. In the fall of 1980, with the first Chinese trade exhibition going on in San Francisco, Kirk immediately grabbed the opportunity. He held conversations with the Chinese and U.S. organizers of the show. He then talked with leaders of the China Council for the Promotion of International Trade and China Exhibition Corporation and discussed with them the possibility of bringing a Chinese trade show to Seattle. At the same time, Kirk's Trade Fair was actively supporting a number of Washington firms to participate in the first U.S. trade exhibition scheduled to open later that fall in Beijing.

Still, I couldn't resist asking Kirk the obvious question. How does he reconcile the fact that he fought the Chinese in the Korean War and the fact that he helped found the Council to promote trade and relations with the Chinese?

Kirk's answer? "I was a professional soldier." To that already perfect answer he then added, "The world changed. I changed with it."

Richard L. Kirk, 2005

1.8

High Five—Incorporating It!

If spring is the time for new lease on life, it must also be the time for new ideas.

With the normalization of diplomatic relations between the United States and China in January, Deng Xiaoping's visit to Seattle in February, the Liu Lin Hai's docking in Elliott Bay in April, WCIT's China mission in May, Mayor Charles Royer's trip to China in June, and Governor Ray's visit to China and Seattle-Shanghai friendship port agreement expected in fall, the spring of 1979 in Seattle was a time of special ferment.

Indeed, an idea was fermenting—the idea of an organization on China.

After Deng Xiaoping had gone home from visiting Seattle in February, Mr. Robert Anderson and Gov. Dixy Lee Ray began discussing the possibility of forming a non-government and non-profit organization directly involved in dealing with China.

At the Port of Seattle, James Dwyer was thinking along similar lines. Based on his own direct dealing with the Chinese during the Liu Lin Hai's call and his visit to China, he told me, he had become very impressed with the Chinese as a talented, enterprising people with great potential. There should be a council, he thought, focused on relations with China, not just business relations, but also cultural and educational relations.

Dwyer said he sat down with Barer one day. "Over a beer?" I asked. "Perhaps over a beer," he laughed while recalling. The two friends discussed the need for such an organization. Maybe because of the beer, or the number of years gone by, neither Dwyer nor Barer remembered the date or place of their meeting. But each remembered its content.

One person who also talked about such an idea was Richard Ford, executive director of the Port of Seattle. Among the people he talked to was Mayor Royer who had just visited China with the U.S. Conference of Mayors. Ford was also ready to lend his support to such an organization. When Dwyer and Barer talked to him about it, Ford said, great, go ahead. Ms. Baillargeon, who had worked under Ford, remembered so, too. She spoke of her former boss as someone who could see the big picture. It was Ford, she said, who encouraged her, as well as Dwyer, to help develop the council on China.

Ms. Baillargeon also emphasized to me that Mr. Roger N. Christiansen had been another major player in starting the Council. Mr. Christiansen was then senior vice president and manager of the China Development Department at the Seattle-First National Bank. He later also served a one-year term as the president of the Council.

I had set out to answer the question "Who exactly came up with the idea of a China council?" The "who" now seemed to turn out plural rather than single. I decided that instead of pursuing a more accurate answer, like "who first?" I would be happy to settle for a better answer: "Great minds think alike."

Still, even if the idea of a China council had been brewing among a number of minds that spring, it fell upon three of the founders, Anderson, Barer and Dwyer, to make the first move towards turning it into reality.

Since the Washington Council on International Trade, or WCIT, had been an important player in international trade in Washington State and Dr. George Taylor, its president, an iconic figure—even nicknamed the "Dean of International Trade,"[70]—our three gentlemen decided that it was necessary that they meet Dr. Taylor about their idea of a council on China.

Dr. Taylor was very gracious, Barer recalled, but not particularly warm to the idea. You know, Taylor said, we already have a relationship with China. Trade with Taiwan is a very important part of the Washington Council on International Trade.

Trade with Taiwan?

Originally from England, educated in both England and United States, Dr. Taylor had spent the better part of the 1930s in China, first as a student, then as

---

70. WCIT, "How Did WCIT Happen?" http://www.wcit.org/resources/publications/ pdfs_pubs/25_years.pdf.

a professor of history in both Beijing and Nanjing. In 1937, Taylor became active in helping the Chinese with the resistance movement against Japan, so active that he had to leave China the following year upon being discovered by the Japanese.[71] That was when Taylor joined the University of Washington where he was to develop its Department of Oriental Studies into an institute.

It is not clear if Dr. Taylor felt partial to Taiwan since the China he had lived in was under the Nationalists, or if he fully embraced the normalization between U.S. and China. It is also hard for the three founders to pinpoint the date of their meeting with Dr. Taylor more than 25 years earlier, whether it was before or after WCIT's May 1979 mission to China of which Taylor was a part. But it would be perfectly understandable if Taylor had reservations about moving too quickly in developing trade relations with China. After all, he was known to have warned the Seattle business community to "temper its heady anticipation about the China trade"[72] back then.

In an interview in March 1979, Dr. Taylor expressed his agreement, on one hand, with a local importer of Chinese agricultural-based goods that in a few years, the Chinese would be able to market more finished goods such as electronics, cameras, tape recorders, television sets, etc. On the other, he expressed fear that the Chinese might dump large quantities of inexpensive goods on the American market, taking customers away from Japan, South Korea and Taiwan. His view was that the resumption of trade relations might be beneficial to China but not to the United States nor to its Asian allies.[73]

It was with these reservations that Dr. Taylor responded to the idea of an organization on China, citing WCIT's good record with Taiwan.

To that, Barer responded, we are not talking about Taiwan. We are talking about the People's Republic of China. Your organization has not been active in that area. Since this is a new relationship, just developing, we think there ought

---

71. Felicia J. Hecker, "International Studies at the University of Washington The First Ninety Years," http://jsis.artsci.washington.edu/jackson/history.html
72. Glenn R. Pascall, "As Asian economic boom slows, NW should adjust," *Puget Sound Business Journal*, Dec. 13, 1996
73. William Trombley, "Seattle Puts Out Welcome Mat for China," *LA Times*, Mar. 12, 1979, p.2

to be an organization devoted just to that subject, because it is such an important relationship in the long run.

Dwyer also remembered how Dr. Taylor objected to the idea of a council for China. As he recalled, Dr. Taylor felt that everything should be under WCIT. Dwyer suggested, OK, then have a special China council under the Washington Council on International Trade. Taylor said no. If we do that, Taylor continued, we should also do it for Russia and some other countries, too.

Since the Seattle Chamber of Commerce was the largest and most influential business organization in western Washington, with the Port of Seattle as a member of the Chamber and Barer being the Chamber's vice president for trade and transportation at the time, our three gentlemen met with the Chamber, too.

The Chamber did not embrace the idea, either. The three gentlemen were warned about funding. They were told that if they were going to form a separate council for China, they would receive no funding from business. As Dwyer told me, they were strongly encouraged not to do it.

But it was not approval from either the WCIT or the Chamber that our founders were seeking, only understanding. Encouragement would have been better. But discouragement wouldn't have changed their mind. They were going to form their own council, a council on China. And they were going to raise money for it, too.

As certain as the spring turning into summer, the idea of a China council was ready to fly, too. No more discussions, no more meetings, no more waiting. It was time to put thoughts on paper.

There may have been more people who had shared or supported the idea of forming a council on China, but destiny had it that five people were going to actually form it.

On the first day of August 1979, four men and one woman, our High Five founders—or signers as Ms. Baillargeon suggested—Mr. Robert C. Anderson, Ms. Patricia M. Baillargeon, Mr. Stanley H. Barer, Mr. James D. Dwyer and Mr. Richard L. Kirk—got together and appeared in person before a notary public in Kirkland. By turns, they put their names on the document, the "Articles of Incorporation of Washington State China Relations Council," each in his or her own forceful and purposeful cursive style. Beside their names were their addresses.

Solemnly, their Articles of Incorporation started:

> "We, the undersigned persons, acting as the incorporators of a corporation under the provisions of the Washington Nonprofit Corporation Act (Revised Code of Washington Ch. 24.03), adopt the following articles of incorporation for such corporation:
>
> Article I.
>
> The name of the corporation shall be WASHINGTON STATE CHINA RELATIONS COUNCIL.
>
> Article II.
>
> The period of duration of the corporation shall be perpetual.
>
> Article III.
>
> a.   The primary purposes of this corporation are as follows:
>
>   1.   To unite in a common effort those persons, entities and organizations engaged in the arts, education, communications, labor, agriculture, industry, transportation, business and trade, for the purpose of monitoring, facilitating, promoting, encouraging, and realizing the enhancement of relations, understanding, goodwill and friendship between the peoples of the State of Washington and the peoples of the People's Republic of China…" [74]

Reading the document, I could almost feel the great sense of mission the founders must have felt that day. It somehow made me think of another group of people putting their fingerprints on a handwritten document about eight months before in China, in December of 1978.

It was a group of 18 peasants of the Xiaogang Village of Fengyang County of Anhui Province. Out of desperate poverty, they pledged in secrecy, risking jail terms, to start working the public plots on a family contract system. They didn't go to jail. In fact, they started what Deng Xiaoping soon promoted to the whole of China: the rural reform represented by the Family Responsibility System.

---

74.   Washington State China Relations Council archives.

The five founders of course didn't have to sign onto the Council in secrecy. But to be the first to do something, as the first person that ate a crab in a Chinese saying, always necessitates courage, determination, and vision as well as risk of failure or setback. In that sense, the five founders were brave trailblazers.

On August 6, Bruce K. Chapman, the secretary of state of Washington who went on to become an assistant to President Reagan, U.S. ambassador to U.N. Organizations in Vienna and now president of the Discovery Institute in Seattle, signed and affixed the seal of the State of Washington on the incorporation certificate of the Washington State China Relations Council and filed it for record in his office. With that, the Council was officially born. Not only was it the first council that focused on relations with China in Washington state, it was also the first such organization in all fifty states of America, and the only one for many years to come.

Mr. Anderson was right that the Council was formed because a number of factors, the right time, right place and right people. The right time was, of course, the normalization of the U.S.-China relations and Deng Xiaoping's visit. The right place was Washington state with its favorable mix of products, facilities, and location as well as history of trade. The right people were Sens. Magnuson and Jackson, Gov. Ray, the five founders and all their supporters. It coincides with the Chinese belief that good things happen when there is a combination of good timing, favorable location and harmonious people.

But why August 1st? Why August? I asked. The founders could not recall. But August, being the 8th month, is considered a lucky one in Chinese culture just because of the pronunciation of eight rhymes with that of prosperity. Inadvertently, the founders made sure the Council would thrive.

And why the name "Washington State China Relations Council?" I also asked. It sounded governmental. Mr. Barer explained it this way. At that time you know, he said, the Chinese preferred dealing with governmental organizations to private ones. Yes, indeed. I should have known that. The ambiguity, he emphasized, was intended. Ms. Baillargeon gave me similar explanations.

Ten days later, on Aug. 17, the incorporating board of directors of the Washington State China Relations Council—the five founders—held its first organizational meeting. Anderson served as the chairman of the meeting, and Barer the secretary. Before the Council had its own office, the founders were going to have the first few meetings, including this one, in Anderson's Seattle office as a temporary location.

They first elected the Council officers, with Anderson as the president of and Baillargeon as the secretary-treasurer. They then elected the interim executive committee, comprising the five of them. They agreed to seek additional members for the board of directors. They also adopted the Council bylaws. And in the end, very importantly, they discussed the necessity of obtaining discretionary funds in the amount of $15,000 from the Pacific Northwest Regional Council,[75] a body of regional governments in those years supporting each other's economic development initiatives. The task of applying for the funds was given to Anderson.

Meanwhile, Dwyer, using his own skills and connections, had been raising money among businesses. He had talked to the port, his employer. He had also talked to two gentlemen who had been to China with him that May, Andrew V. Smith, president of Pacific Northwest Bell Telephone Company and William M. Jenkins, chairman of Seattle-First National Bank. Each of them agreed to support the Council with at least $10,000.

On November 2, 1979, the Board of Directors of Washington State China Relations held a special meeting. Anderson served as the chairman, and Robert A. Kapp, a young assistant professor of Chinese history at the University of Washington's School of International Studies, served as the secretary. The first order of business was the election of an executive director. That important, and historic, order of business was recorded this way:

> "The Chairman advised Robert Kapp had agreed to accept the position of Executive Director, with the understanding that so long as he is teaching at the University of Washington the amount of time he contributes to the Council will be limited to one full day per week, plus miscellaneous lunches and dinners. After discussion, upon motion duly made, seconded and unanimously carried, the Board of Directors elected Robert Kapp to serve as Executive Director of the Washington State China Relations Council."[76]

---

75. Ibid.
76. Ibid.

From that day on and in the years to come, Kapp, the first executive director of the Council, played a prominent role not only at the Washington State China Relations Council, but also at the Washington Council on International Trade (WCIT); and, not only in Washington state, but also in Washington D.C. His extraordinary story, however, will be reserved for Part II.

The meeting went on. Anderson reported on the approval of the $15,000 grant from the Pacific Northwest Regional Council and advised on the offer by the State Department of Commerce and Economic Development of the temporary use of its Seattle office space near Seattle Center to the Council. The interim executive committee—the five incorporating board of directors—then drew up a slate of persons to be invited to join the board. Anderson again reported that the entire Washington State Congressional Delegation, the governor of the State of Washington, the mayor of Seattle, and the mayor of Spokane had already agreed to serve as ex officio members of the board of directors.

With a newly elected executive director in Mr. Kapp, with funding coming in, with office space secured, with an impressive body of ex officio board members already signed up, and with a new slate of directors ready to join, the founders took up the last, but not the least, item of on the agenda: planning the timing and mechanics of "going public." That order of business was recorded this way:

> "There was a general agreement that the Council should make its existence known in the near future, and in the best-organized and most auspicious manner possible…The Council will make its existence known formally as soon as the full Board is assembled, ideally by the second week of December, 1979…"[77]

With that, our High Five founders and the first executive director were ready to let the newly formed Washington State China Relations Council meet the world, and in style.

---

77.   Ibid.

STATE OF WASHINGTON | DEPARTMENT OF STATE

D291394
FILE NUMBER

DOMESTIC

I, **BRUCE K. CHAPMAN**, Secretary of State of the State of Washington and custodian of its seal, hereby certify that

ARTICLES OF INCORPORATION

of_____WASHINGTON STATE CHINA RELATIONS COUNCIL_____

a domestic corporation of_____Seattle,____Washington,

was filed for record in this office on this date, and I further certify that such Articles remain on file in this office.

In witness whereof I have signed and have affixed the seal of the State of Washington to this certificate at Olympia, the State Capitol,

August 6, 1979

BRUCE K. CHAPMAN
SECRETARY OF STATE

(Washington State China Relations Council archives.)

1.9

The Grand Opening

The time was January 3rd, 1980, a Thursday. The place was the Westin Hotel in Seattle. The event: the Washington State China Relations Council's first news conference to announce its establishment officially to the public.

It was two days after the anniversary of the normalization of diplomatic relations between the United States and China on January 1, 1979, and one month shy of the anniversary of Vice Premier Deng Xiaoping's visit to Seattle in early February of 1979. If the founders and the executive director had been preparing the Council's "going public" in time to celebrate both anniversaries, they succeeded.

Since the board meeting back in November 1979, the Council not only had all the directors ex officio signed on, it had also put together an illustrious panel of directors. All together, the Council's Board of Directors read like who's who of Washington state:

Directors Ex Officio

The Honorable Warren G. Magnuson, United States Senator
The Honorable Henry M. Jackson, United States Senator
The Honorable Don Bonker, Member of Congress
The Honorable Norm Dicks, Member of Congress
The Honorable Thomas S. Foley, Member of Congress
The Honorable Mike Lowry, Member of Congress
The Honorable Mike McCormack, Member of Congress
The Honorable Joel M. Pritchard, Member of Congress
The Honorable Al Swift, Member of Congress
The Honorable Dixy Lee Ray, Governor
The Honorable Ron Bair, Mayor, City of Spokane
The Honorable Mike Parker, Mayor, City of Tacoma
The Honorable Charles Royer, Mayor, City of Seattle
Mr. Merle D. Adlum, President, Port of Seattle Commission
Mr. L.T. Pepin, President, Washington Public Ports Association

Directors

Robert C. Anderson, Director, Washington State Department of Commerce and Economic Development

Patricia Baillargeon, Trade Consultant

Stanley H. Barer, Attorney at Law, Houger, Garvey, Schubert, Adams and Barer

James D. Dwyer, Senior Director, Port Development and Relations, Port of Seattle

Richard L. Kirk, Executive Director, Washington State International Trade Fair

William P. Gerberding, President, University of Washington

William N. Gross, Senior Vice President, PACCAR, Inc.

Scott Hanson, Administrator, Washington Wheat Commission, Spokane

Bob J. Mickelson, Director, Washington Department of Agriculture

Harry Mullikin, President and Chief Executive Officer, Western International Hotels

William L. Hamilton, Vice President-Planning and International Business, The Boeing Company

William M. Jenkins, Chairman, Seattle-First National Bank

Jon M. Lindbergh, Vice President, DOMSEA Farms Inc.

Wendell J. Satre, President and Chairman of the Board, Washington Water Power Company

Andrew V. Smith, President, Pacific Northwest Bell

Walter E. Schoenfeld, President, Schoenfeld Industries Inc.

Melvin M. Stewart, President, Seattle Stevedore Co.

Dr. Glenn Terrell, President, Washington State University

G. Robert Truex, Jr., Chairman, Rainier National Bank

Jackson Tse, President, EST Industries

Dr. L. Van Citters, Dean, University of Washington School of Medicine

George H. Weyerhaeuser, President, Weyerhaeuser Company[78]

Mr. Anderson, the Council president, was the first to speak to the gathering of local business and civic leaders as well as the media:

> "After 30 years of hostility and broken communications, this nation's diplomatic relations with the People's Republic of China have now been restored.

---

78. Washington State China Relations Council archives.

"Since the end of 1976, the PRC has embarked on a new course of political and economic development and is making major efforts to look abroad for cooperation with other countries in its modernization drive.

"The Washington State China Relations Council will attempt to work with the Chinese in such fields as transportation, medicine, agriculture and telecommunications.

"The WSCRC will also help facilitate visits by Chinese individuals and organizations to Washington state, and act as a liaison with government and private agencies.

"Our location can enable us to funnel a healthy share of the nation's China trade through Washington. In the years to come, this could become a significant factor in the economic life of this state.

"The products and resources of Washington, including not only wheat and aircraft but also high technology, financial services, technical and educational resources, a large Chinese American community, and a historical popular orientation to East Asia, make this state the natural beneficiary of expanding U.S.-China ties."[79]

With those words, Anderson expressed the confidence and hope not only of himself but all his Council comrades and supporters.

Anderson then read the statements respectively from Sen. Magnuson, Sen. Jackson, and Governor Ray.

Sen. Magnuson gave his view of the new organization this way, "The Washington State China Relations Council will be a microcosm of Washington state trade, commerce, cultural and educational interests dedicated to establishing specific economic and cultural ties between our state and the People's Republic of China...I shall continue to do all that I can to support this effort and this organization."[80]

Sen. Jackson expressed pleasure but also suggested caution to the new council, "Because our two nations have been out of contact for a long time and have dif-

---

79. Seattle Daily Journal of Commerce, "State China Relations Council formed," Jan. 4, 1980, p.1
80. Ibid.

ferent historical backgrounds, development of mutually useful relations will not happen automatically. It will take care, patience, good communication and organization. The Washington State China Relations Council should provide those key ingredients."[81]

Governor Ray, in her statement, mentioned Anderson's and her trip to China three months earlier at the invitation of Vice Premier Deng Xiaoping, and said, "We were impressed by China's determination to develop its industry, agriculture, science and technology. I was also impressed that we have much to learn from each other. The formation of the Washington State China Relations Council is an important step toward developing closer working ties in activities of commerce, education and culture between our state and the People's Republic of China."[82]

Following Anderson, a number of directors of the board also spoke. Among them was Harry Mullikin, president of the chain that is now Westin Hotels, who said, "The Council will emphasize the geographic closeness to China, provide a 'focal point' for any business or group seeking information about or closer ties with China and build toward a long-term relationship with the People's Republic."[83]

Mr. Bob Mickelson, director of the state Department of Agriculture, took the floor, too. With the news that the wheat smut problem was being solved, he predicted that state ports would soon be moving large quantities of fresh and processed foods to China.[84]

Also in attendance was Mr. Stanley Young of Washington, D.C., vice president of the National Council for United States-China Trade. Formed in 1973 after Nixon's visit to China, Mr. Young's Council was the predecessor of today's US-China Business Council.

---

81. Ibid.
82. Ibid.
83. Svein Gilje, "State to lead in China trade, says new group," *The Seattle Times*, Jan. 7, 1980, p. A10
84. Jerry Craig, "China expert counsels patience," *Seattle Daily Journal of Commerce*, Jan. 4, 1980

Young talked about special advantages Washington state had over other regions, such as being closest geographically to China. He told the audience that the Chinese appreciated the "gateway concept."[85] He then talked more specifically about two-way trade. The aircraft industry, primarily The Boeing Co., he said, would become the No. 1 export industry to China in 1980. The year before, however, it was yellow corn, wheat, and cotton that had topped American exports to China.[86] The two-way trade total for 1979, Mr. Young said, was estimated at $2 billion.[87] But he emphasized that trade balance had been much more in favor of U.S. exports.

Attending the news conference was also Mr. Brock Adams, now back in law practice after serving two years as President Carter's transportation secretary, and his law partner Stanley Barer, our Liu Lin Hai launcher. The two gentlemen were actually flying to China right after the news conference. They were going to seek business opportunities for their clients in airlines, oil exploration and shipping businesses. They were also bringing with them something special: papers on the Council.

I asked Barer about those papers the two of them took to China. He said they had given all the information on the Council to American Ambassador Leonard Woodcock and asked him to advise all appropriate Chinese entities and officials.

During the news conference, Mr. Kapp, our brand-new executive director, handed out copies of information sheet of the Council. Here is the text.

Introducing

The Washington State China Relations Council

The Purpose:

To develop our state's role as a major Gateway to China by stimulating beneficial relations between the people of Washington and their counterparts in the People's Republic of China.

---

85. Ibid.
86. Ibid.
87. Ibid.

The Reasons:

This state's natural potential for strong China ties; geographic location, agricultural and forest resources, ports and trade facilities, industrial and technological strengths, higher educational institutions, cultural and civic-group interests, heritage of Chinese and Chinese-American contributions.

China's embarkation on programs of massive modernization coupled with increased foreign trade and other forms of communication with the world; China's clearly-expressed interests in learning from foreign experiences and in cultivating joint-venture and other economic relationships.

Normalization of U.S.-China relations; rapid increase in the complexity and variety of U.S.-China contacts; U.S. unfamiliarity with Chinese conditions and Chinese culture and Chinese unfamiliarity with the U.S.

Our state's need for full inclusion in U.S. national China-related activities; the need for an in-state focal point of information and program development regarding relations with China; the need to bring Washington's resources and advantages to Chinese attention; the need to maintain forward momentum in the long-term development of cordial economic and cultural contacts with the people of China.

The Program:

Development of exchanges and visits between Council members and their Chinese counterparts; work with Council members in defining potential interests regarding China; assistance in efforts to bring exhibits, trade shows, cultural presentations; close cooperation with national organizations (National Council for U.S.-China Trade, National Committee on U.S.-China Relations, etc.) to ensure full Washington participation in U.S. visits of major Chinese delegations; seminars and meetings with guests from government, trade, the arts, or other areas of member interests; briefings and updates for Council members traveling to China; informational publications directed to Council members and to appropriate Chinese readers; assistance to members maximizing the impact of Chinese visits to the State of Washington.

The Council:

A non-profit corporation; a twenty-five person Board of Directors selected from among the leaders of Washington agriculture, business, education, labor, arts, the professions, and trade; an Executive Committee of the Board of Directors; an Executive Director. The entire Washington Congressional delegation, the Governor, the Mayors of Seattle, Spokane, Tacoma are Board members ex officio.

The Members:

Individuals; civic, cultural, and educational groups; corporations—from throughout Washington.

Kapp also informed the audience that for office facilities, the Council was using leased space in the Seattle Field Office of the Washington State Department of Commerce and Economic Development at 312 First Avenue North, to keep the expenses minimal.

Mr. Anderson then announced in conclusion, "This is the beginning, but a solid beginning."[88]

With that, the Washington State China Relations Council was officially open for business. It was also starting to write the chronicles of the Washington state-China relations.

The first logo, mailing address and telephone number of the Council.

---

88.   Svein Gilje, "State to lead in China trade, says new group," *The Seattle Times*, Jan. 7, 1980, p. A10

Part II

Directing

Introduction

If the founders of the Washington State China Relations Council were visionary architects who saw the promise to Washington state in the newly normalized U.S.-China relations and put together an organization to fulfill that promise, then the executive directors of the Council were knowledgeable managers who not only had the skills to steward the organization, but also the expertise to develop Washington state-China relations in fulfilling that promise.

As we have seen, the founders of the Washington State China Relations Council, my China Council High Five, were all leading economic and business experts in Washington state, from commerce development to port development, from international trade to international marine transportation. The directors of the Council, on the other hand, have all been established China experts, with academic and/or diplomatic backgrounds, and from all over the country.

A veteran regional business reporter once pointed out in a piece on the Council, "One measure of the state's prominence in the China business was the council's success in attracting top executive directors."[1] I would add that it is also a measure of the Council's prominence in promoting the China business. These "top executive directors" are truly a "cream of the crop" group.

Since its formation in 1979, the Council has had four executive directors. The first was Mr. Robert A. Kapp, followed by Mr. William B. Abnett, Mr. Eden Y. Woon and Mr. Joseph J. Borich, making them my China Council Gang of Four. It is an all male gang, of course, for now at least. We start with Kapp.

---

1.   Stephen Dunphy, "China ties started early, stayed strong," *The Seattle Times*, Jun. 20, 2004

2.1

Robert Kapp—The Pioneer
(Executive Director, 1979–1987 and 1992–1994)

Robert A. Kapp, late 1980s

As its founding and longest-serving executive director, Robert A. Kapp became almost synonymous with the Washington State China Relations Council. When I interviewed the Council founders, one question asked me every time was "Have you talked to Bob Kapp?"

I met Mr. Kapp only once, and briefly. But I have read and heard so much about him that I felt I knew him, without really knowing him.

I had to admit that of all the founders and directors of the Council, I felt most intimidated by Kapp. After serving as the first executive director of the Washington State China Relations Council and then as president of the Washington Council on International Trade (WCIT), Kapp went on to serve as president of the US-China Business Council and became a national figure and voice in the area of U.S.-China business policy. I felt so inadequate to even attempt to write about him. Now I had to "talk" to him. I was nervous.

After I plucked up my courage and sent him the first e-mail, he responded quickly and in a friendly manner. "I'm delighted to try to respond to you anytime if you send me an e-mail with questions," he wrote. I felt better instantly.

When I think of Kapp, I think of the saying "Those who can, do. Those who can't, teach." To me, he is the true embodiment of that saying. I asked him for his response.

Kapp did respond. But he didn't quite like the saying or my observation. He said, "I think that 'teaching' is also a very respectable and honorable form of 'doing,' and that the witticism you quote (an old one) is intellectually flawed." Well, that may be. But I still think that U.S.-China business community, even U.S.-China trade relations, would have suffered had Kapp stayed on in teaching.

Born and raised in the New York City area, young Kapp went to a private school, Swarthmore College, in southeastern Pennsylvania. Thanks to a basic Modern China and Japan history course in his second year, as Kapp told me, he became interested in East Asia. In 1964, he entered the MA program in East Asia Studies at Yale. That was the year Kapp considered the beginning of his involvement with China, as he told an audience years later. There were courses on both China and Japan. But Kapp concentrated on Chinese language, history and related topics from the beginning. After receiving his MA in 1966, he stayed on at Yale, this time, pursuing a Ph.D. in, what else, Modern Chinese History.

After getting his Ph.D in 1970, Kapp immediately joined the faculty of Rice University in Houston. He was responsible for all history courses on China, including a broad survey course and some higher-level modern history courses. Three years later, Kapp was invited to join the faculty of the University of Washington (UW) in Seattle, with a joint appointment in history and in the Institute for Comparative And Foreign Area Studies, which was later the Jackson School of International Studies. Much of his work here as Assistant Professor of History, he said, involved guiding Ph.D students through their course work and their dissertations, though he also taught the modern-China segment of an undergraduate course.

Two of his writings from those years that I found on the Internet give one a feel of Kapp's field of academic concentration. One had the title "The Kuomintang and Rural China in the War of Resistance, 1937–1945,"[2] the other, "Szechwan (the old spelling of Sichuan) and the Chinese Republic: Provincial Militarism and Central Power, 1911–1938."[3] Remember Sichuan, the name of a Chinese province, for it would be a focus again in Kapp's work at the Council.

When Nixon went to China, Kapp was still at Rice University. After he moved to Seattle, it was natural that he and two colleagues would get involved with the Seattle Chapter of the Asia Society's China Council, formed in the mid 1970s and aimed at K-12 education and public understanding of China.

When they learned that Vice Premier Deng Xiaoping would make Seattle the last stop of his early February 1979 visit to the United States, Kapp and his two colleagues shifted into high gear. They made all kinds of media contacts such as telephone interviews, television news spots, and briefings to reporters to explain normalization to the local media and the general public.

To help Seattle in its preparation to receive Vice Premier Deng, Kapp, along with another China specialist friend, also briefed Seattle Mayor Charles Royer and Port of Seattle officials on the correct protocols to utilize with the Chinese. Using a chalkboard, Kapp even taught the port commissioners such Chinese phrases as "welcome", "how are you", "cheers", and "thank you".[4]

Although a family emergency took Kapp away from Seattle when Vice Premier Deng was in town, the brand-new U.S.-China relationship kept his mind busy. He had been thinking about China's ambitious modernization program and the immensity of the task. He had also observed the growing expectation among Washington state businesses of an imminent boon of China trade in the Northwest. He talked to the press about his observation the day before Deng's arrival.

---

2.   http://www.ewtn.com/library/HOMELIBR/FR89102.TXT

3.   http://library.nps.navy.mil/home/bibs/yangtzebooks.htm

4.   Erin Van Bronkhorst, "A Protocol Hint: No Jokes," *Seattle Post-Intelligencer*, Feb. 3, 1979

With 80 per cent of the population still involved in agriculture, Kapp said:

> "...the Chinese have a tremendously long way to go in virtually every segment of their economy. The human problems of administering such a society and its very rapid changes are enormously complex and overwhelming. It's really the transformation of the whole society. Its uncharted water and the ramifications of all this modernization are unclear."[5]

As an expert on China's modern history, Kapp, in fact, was calling attention to the reality of China at the time.

Kapp knew that reality not only because of his study of China's modern history, he knew it also from a trip he had just taken to China in January 1977, only several months after the death of Mao. Recalling that first trip to China, he wrote of his impression in an email,

> "Drabness...A sense of the immediacy of the trauma just past...The tentativeness of all Chinese assigned to deal with foreigners at this early stage. The decrepitude of the physical infrastructure, lack of maintenance of buildings, transportation facilities...The limitation of food availability in the markets...The poignancy of a meeting at Beida (Beijing University) with Zhou Peiyuan (the Beida president) and other university figures who had survived the storms that had engulfed them..."

It was exactly that knowledge of China's reality that the Council's founders saw as Kapp's major qualification for the position of executive director.

I asked Kapp about the ending of his teaching career. He was very frank: "My future at the University of Washington was, to put it mildly, 'uncertain.'"

But by throwing in with the business leaders to get the Washington State China Relations Council going, Kapp chose instead an even bigger uncertainty, not just with regard to the Council, but the whole U.S.-China relationship.

We can all applaud Kapp, after the fact, for making that decision in the fall of 1979. From then on, in building Washington State-China relations, Kapp

---

5.   Richard Buck, "Port of Seattle looking to share of China trade," *The Seattle Times,* Feb. 4, 1979, p. B6

became the one who could, and did. But before he did it full time, Kapp was only on a "one full day per week, plus miscellaneous lunches and dinners"[6] basis at the Council. It was not until the end of the spring quarter in 1980 that Kapp would complete his service at the UW. He was to start full time at the Council on October 1, 1980.[7]

But even on part-time basis, Kapp began in February 1980 to start the first membership drive. At the end of the first quarter of CY 1980, there were 17 member firms. By the end of the second, there were already 27. In the fall, the number increased to 37. By the end of the year, it reached almost 50.[8] Reading the newsletter written by Kapp at the time, one could feel the excitement he must have experienced with the success of the Council's first membership drive.

> "During 1980, the Council developed its membership from zero to nearly fifty firms and public agencies. The Council's members range from single-owner proprietorship to the largest economic entities in the state. It will be clear from the attached list of members that some firms have direct business relations with China already, but that others support the Council out of a broader concern for the economic and cultural vitality of Washington State."[9]

The list Kapp attached to the newsletter started with The Boeing Company and ended with Weyerhaeuser Company. The two, along with many other Washington state businesses and institutions, were to remain on the list ever since.

In the summer of 1980, the Council had also moved into its own permanent quarters. As Kapp happily informed members in the fall newsletter, which he now named "Council News,"

> "After six start-up months in the Seattle Field Office building of the Washington State Department of Commerce and Economic Development, the WSCRC established offices in Pioneer Square, Seattle, in July. The Council's new address is 360 Grand Central on the Park, 216 First Avenue South. The phone number remains 464–1409."[10]

---

6.   Washington State China Relations Council archives.
7.   Ibid.
8.   Washington State China Relations Council newsletter, Feb.17, 1981
9.   Ibid.
10. Washington State China Relations Council, *"Council News,"* Fall 1980

In the same newsletter, Kapp urged members to visit, browse the informational material and talk to the staff, which now included Kapp himself and administrative assistant Anna Manis Tabor.

From whence came the Chinese name of the Council and the beautiful calligraphic rendering of it in the Council's logo and stationary that was used for nearly twenty years?

Kapp told me that the calligraphy was by a gentleman named Karl Lo, then Director of the East Asia Library of the University of Washington, who also helped him develop the Chinese name of the Council. Mr. Lo was still active, Kapp said, but now at University of California at San Diego.

At Kapp's suggestion, I sent Mr. Lo an email. Friendly and still with a good memory, Lo replied that he and Kapp had indeed exchanged ideas on how to translate the terms "Washington" and "Relations" so as to avoid confusion with Washington D.C. and federal government connections. He also admitted designing the calligraphy, but with a good dose of humility. Lo emphasized the "humility" with a smiley. It was mainly because, he said, there was no Chinese typesetting machine in town at the time. Also, the two of them thought personal handwriting conveyed a friendlier image than typesetting. It did indeed.

Not only with the calligraphy, Kapp and Lo also did a really good job with the Council's Chinese name, which literally reads "Washington State China Exchange Council." It successfully avoided the confusion of the word "relations" which could convey the notion of a diplomatic connection between Washington State and China.

September 1980, one month before Kapp started working for the Council full time, turned out to be a busy one right from the start. Kapp had just returned on August 29 from a month-long trip to China, serving as the resident China specialist for a Smithsonian Institution associates group. On September 1, the Chinese Vice Premier Bo Yibo, one of China's most senior economic planners, and his 16-member delegation from China's State Machine Building Industry Commission were already in Seattle. The group was in the U.S. as the guests of the National Council for U.S.-China Trade, predecessor of the US-China Business Council. After visiting Seattle, including the Boeing facilities, Vice Premier Bo was going to San Francisco to open the first Chinese trade exhibition in the U.S.

and Washington D.C. to co-chair the first meeting of the U.S.-China Joint Economic Committee.

Kapp, on behalf of the Washington State China Relations Council, gave his first high-level banquet that evening. Attending the banquet was Christopher H. Philips, President of the National Council for U.S.-China Trade, Sen. and Mrs. Magnuson, Mayor and Mrs. Royer, Council president and Mrs. Anderson and 75 local business and financial leaders. Chinese Ambassador to the United States Chai Zemin was there, too.

Vice Premier Bo gave warm remarks at the banquet:

> "...the position of Seattle in the development of economic relations and friendly trends with our country is an important one. This is the American city nearest our country, and an important port...It goes without saying: Seattle is a very important gateway for Sino-U.S. economic intercourse and for the channels of friendship between the two countries.

> "Since the formation of the Washington State China Relations Council...the Council has performed a great deal of highly effective work. We look forward to the Council's achieving even greater results in the future.

> "Today, we have been delighted to meet Sen. Magnuson...As far back as the 1950s, Sen. Magnuson favored trade with the People's Republic of China and advocated the development of diplomatic relations. The correctness of his position has been proved by history..."[11]

Later that month, at the invitation of Vice Premier Bo's group, Kapp went down to San Francisco and joined the Chinese for some of the opening festivities of the Chinese trade show.

Back in Seattle, Kapp began working on the structure of the Council's future programs and activities. To maximize effective cooperation among members with related interest, he initiated the establishing of the Council's technical committees. The committees, organized as follows, would help guide the Council programming, initiate activities of particular concern to their members, and act as principal hosts for Chinese visitors according to their areas of expertise:

---

11.   Washington State China Relations, *"Council News,"* Fall 1980

Agribusiness Technical Committee
Banking Technical Committee
Consulting Services Technical Committee
Cultural Affairs Technical Committee
Education Technical Committee
Forest Products Technical Committee
Import Assistance Technical Committee
Manufacturing Technical Committee
Medical Affairs Technical Committee
Professional Services Technical Committee (Law, Financial Services, Insurance)
Transportation Technical Committee[12]

With the Council off to a great start, Kapp did not forget to further inform the Washington state public of the new relations with China as well as the new organization. In the December 1980 issue of Puget Soundings, Kapp wrote an essay titled "Washington State Meets China." In it, one could see his typical realistic views:

"Normalization in 1979 opened new opportunities—and posed new risks. The restoration of normal economic dealings augured well for the state's role, both as a transshipment center for the nation's imports and exports and as a production center for products needed in China's modernization. Yet pitfalls remained; one of the most serious being ill-informed over-enthusiasm…What was needed was information and realism, not rumors and daydreams."[13]

That's why the public needed to learn about the Washington State China Relations Council, as Kapp continued:

"The Council's activities fall into two rough categories. First, the Council assists firms in their dealings with China by providing information, background, language assistance, and other forms of advice. Second, the Council exposes the state and the Council members to their Chinese counterparts and visitors with maximum effectiveness."[14]

---

12. Washington State China Relations Council newsletter, Feb. 17, 1981
13. Robert Kapp, "Washington State Meets China," *Puget Soundings*, Dec. 1980
14. Ibid.

Not just to Chinese counterparts and visitors, Kapp had something else in mind to which he would expose the Washington state public as well as the Council members—Sichuan.

In the spring of 1980, Kapp had reported in the Council newsletter on the development of Sichuan as well as its Party Secretary Zhao Ziyang. He wrote about how Sichuan was a large, productive and populous province, but had suffered impoverishment during the Cultural Revolution, and how Zhao Ziyang turned things around by carrying out rural reforms and bringing leftist excesses under control.[15] It was true that Zhao Ziyang's rural reforms were so successful that people in Sichuan had a jingle for him, "Want rice? Look for Ziyang." Kapp tried also to draw the attention of the Council members to the fact that because of his success, Zhao Ziyang had just been promoted to the State Council to be the Acting Premier.

In the same newsletter, Kapp also wrote for the first time an eye-catching subtitle "State-to-Province Relationship." Underneath, Kapp informed the members that at the suggestion of the Council, Gov. Dixy Lee Ray had sent a request to Vice Premier Deng Xiaoping for his assistance in starting the ball rolling toward a Washington-Sichuan relationship. He concluded, with confidence:

> "It is anticipated that the Council will manage the Washington State side of this relationship as it emerges."[16]

In September, Kapp was ready to move the ball faster. First he sent a telegraph to the Chinese Friendship Association Sichuan Branch, formally suggesting the establishment of friendship relations. Then he, as well as Mr. Robert Anderson, president of the Council, followed up with a number of inquiries and correspondence with the Chinese.

In March 1981, Kapp organized and accompanied a five-day visit of the vice governor of Sichuan, Mr. Mou Haixiu, to Washington, D.C, with an intensive round of activities there including visiting the White House, the State Department, and the Department of Commerce. In June, Council president for that year, Mr. Roger N. Christiansen, who was senior vice president and manager of

---

15. Washington State China Relations Newsletter Spring Quarter 1980
16. Ibid.

the China Development Department, Seattle First National Bank, led a small delegation, including Kapp, to Sichuan, exploring the issues of economic, technological and cultural exchanges between Washington State and Sichuan Province. In October, Kapp met in New York with Lu Dadong, governor of Sichuan, and Zhou Shangqing, director of the general affairs department of the Sichuan provincial party committee. By November, Governor John D. Spellman of Washington and Governor Lu Dadong of Sichuan had exchanged letters, confirming each side's interest in such a relationship.

To pave the way for formal relations and to establish ties in China for the Council, Kapp made another trip to Sichuan plus Beijing and Shanghai in April and May 1982. Two months later, in June, Li Xinfu, deputy secretary-general of Sichuan provincial government and director of its foreign affairs office, came to Seattle. It was during this visit that the plans were made for Gov. Spellman to visit Sichuan in October to finalize the sister state-province relationship.

On August 7, 1982, the Office of the Governor of the State of Washington issued this news release:

> "Governor John Spellman announced today that he will lead a delegation of Washington State leaders on a friendship and trade mission to the People's Republic of China as the guest of the government of Sichuan Province.

> "The highlight of the mission will be the signing of an agreement establishing a formal friendly relationship between Sichuan and Washington State.

> "'The purpose of this mission is to formalize and to strengthen further existing friendly ties between our state, the People's Republic of China and Sichuan Province. We expect to achieve a better understanding of China's most populous province and of how we can improve our trading and cultural relations with the People's Republic,' the governor said."[17]

Governor Spellman, in the announcement, did not forget to give credit to the Council:

---

17.   Washington State Archives.

"The 'sister state' friendship agreement was negotiated by the state Department of Commerce and Economic Development with major assistance from the Washington State China Relations Council…"[18]

In his September 13, 1982, newsletter to the members and directors of the Council, Kapp wrote, with great excitement,

"Most of you have probably heard by now that Governor Spellman is leading a delegation to the People's Republic of China for a visit from October 5 to October 18.

"The visit is at the invitation of the governor of Sichuan Province, Lu Dadong. During the visit, the two governors will formally establish the 'friendship relations between Washington State and Sichuan Province which have been in preparation for over two years.

"The Washington State China Relations Council's long efforts to build this relationship are thus bearing fruit. The Council has been pleased to cooperate with the governor and other state leaders in building this tie with a major Chinese provincial counterpart. We will continue to play a key role in cooperative projects once the relationship is in place…"[19]

On October 10, Gov. Spellman arrived in Sichuan. With him was an impressive 32-member delegation made up of state government officials as well as leaders from Washington state's agricultural, commercial, foreign trade and education sectors, half of them Council members, including The Boeing Company, the University of Washington and Weyerhaeuser Company. Stanley Barer, one of the five founders, was the Council's principal representative on the mission and served as the group's general counsel. Kapp was, of course, part of the official delegation.

The next day, October 11, 1982, at the Jin Niu (Golden Ox) Hotel in Chengdu, capital of Sichuan Province, Gov. John Spellman and Gov. Lu Dadong signed the agreement formally establishing friendship relations between Washington State and Sichuan Province.

---

18. Ibid.
19. Washington State Archives.

James Dwyer, who served as the president of the Council in 1982, put the sister relationship on top of the major achievements and events of the year in the annual report:

> "Establishment of formal relations of friendship between Washington State and Sichuan, during Governor Spellman's mission to China (October, 1982)
>
> Visit of Sichuan Provincial Delegation to Washington State (June, 1982)
>
> Expanded sales of forest products to China throughout the year;
>
> The sale of Boeing 737s and 747s to China in late 1982;
>
> Physio-Control's conclusion of the largest single sale in its history, to China in October;"[20]
>
> ...

A year later, in September 1983, the year Stanley Barer served as the president of the Council, then Governor Yang Xizong of Sichuan and his friendship delegation along with a trade and economic team from the province, visited Washington to reciprocate the visit to Sichuan by Gov. Spellman and the Washington delegation. The Sichuan delegation toured Washington state, conducted meetings, and planned trade exhibitions, agricultural exchanges and educational contacts. The sister state relationship was now in full bloom.

How did Kapp feel about the new sister state relationship with Sichuan? The fall 1982 issue of the "Council News" saw Kapp's joy overflowing. He began this way: "Washington State has a new and very big Friend in China..."[21] He continued,

> "Formal establishment of Friendship Relations between Washington and Sichuan marked the climax of several years of effort by the two sides..."[22]

What Kapp did not mention was that the Washington-Sichuan relationship was not only the first major achievement of the Council, but also the first major

---

20.   Washington State China Relations Council archives
21.   Washington State China Relations Council, *"Council News,"* Fall 1982
22.   Ibid.

achievement of Kapp himself as its executive director. It firmly established the Council as what it had been incorporated and named to do—building Washington state-China relations. It also firmly established Kapp as a capable pioneering executive director of the Council.

Furthermore, the relationship with Sichuan not only benefited Washington state companies and institutions through the cultural, educational and commercial exchanges to come, it also spawned another relationship: the sister-city relationship between Seattle and Chongqing in 1983.

But why Sichuan, out of all 29 provinces of China? It was of course not just because of its being the largest province, its reputation as the "heavenly storehouse" from its productive land, its gorges and ports on the Yangtze River, and its many mountain peaks, in common with Washington state. I was keenly interested in Kapp's account of the reasons for this history-making relationship.

Kapp wrote this way, "Sichuan was a vitally important province in the early years of post-Cultural Revolution reform, both because of Zhao Ziyang's agricultural experiments there and because of Deng's Xiaoping's deep roots there."

I continued my query, this time focusing on his "personal connection" to Sichuan. Kapp gave in, but just a little: "I also had a fairly strong familiarity with the basic facts of Sichuan's history and economics."

Sichuan was indeed a perfect choice, not only for Washington state, but also for any American state. First, there was Deng Xiaoping, a native son of Sichuan, visiting the U.S. and generating an interest in the province. Then there was Zhao Ziyang, the Sichuan party secretary and later Chinese premier, and his successful reforms, which increased Sichuan's fame. Not to be excluded here were the Sichuan people, history, natural resources, and industries, all of which made Sichuan very attractive.

It was, in fact, so attractive that three other American states beside Washington had been coveting it. One of them was Michigan whose governor William Milliken arrived in Sichuan only a couple of weeks after Gov. Spellman.[23] He

---

23. *The Wall Street Journal*, "U.S. States, Chinese Provinces Starting 'Sister' Relationships," Sept. 7, 1982, p. 29

was, of course, disappointed. That Washington state got Sichuan, to a large extent, was because of the Washington State China Relations Council, and especially because of the early work and quick thinking of Kapp, a China and Sichuan expert. It was a big coup for Washington state, and a big coup for Kapp.

Now with the sister state relationship on track, Kapp had settled in with the Council's more "routine" work such as receiving Chinese delegations visiting Washington, assisting American delegations going to China, briefing American embassy officials returning from Beijing, acquainting Chinese diplomats with Washington state, providing member firms with information on China, giving them advice and assistance in their contacts with China, hosting dinners, organizing luncheons, endorsing China related events, and supporting China-related programs, to name but some aspects.

Helping Kapp with all this was the new administrative assistant Linda Eng, who had joined the Council in spring of 1981 replacing an earlier administrative assistant. But Ms. Eng was not just another administrative assistant, even though she was working on a part-time basis that spring. She was to be the longest-serving administrative assistant of the Council, through two directorships. She would also work for Kapp for many years, at the Council in this Washington and at the US-China Business Council in the other Washington. For Linda, Kapp had one word, "Splendid."

One major and successful effort Kapp made in 1983 was the convening of the Council's first annual fall China trade conference called "China Trade Update 1983." The one-day event presented panels of specialists in China-related fields including politics, economics, technology transfer, law, import and export. It drew one hundred participants. Presenting China's recent political and economic trends were Dr. Thomas Fingar, director of Stanford University's U.S.-China Relations Program, Gao Weijie, president of China Ocean Shipping Co. (Cosco) and the Council's own Kapp. The panels dealt with fields such as importing from China and producing in China for U.S. markets; technology transfer and technology absorption in China; and legal and financial agency support. The scope and attendance so exceeded Council's expectations, Kapp wrote in the newsletter afterwards, that "the Council plans to offer a major event of this type as a regular annual feature of its programming."[24] It did. There was "China Trade Update

---

24. Washington State China Relations Council, *"Council News,"* Fall 1983

1984," with more than 130 participants; "China Trade Update 1985," with more than 150; and "China Trade Update 1986," each more successful than the previous one.

Another very successful event that took place with the Council's endorsement and the Council members' contributions was the six-month exhibition from March 1, 1984, at the Pacific Science Center in Seattle of "China: 7,000 Years of Discovery." Originally organized for display in Toronto, the exhibition ended up in Seattle because of months of negotiations, ultimately successful, between the Pacific Science Center and the China Association for Science and Technology, as well as the Council's help in securing a grant from the state for the Pacific Science Center. It also indicated, as Kapp wrote in a newsletter, "...every sign of being the focal point for a broad array of China-focused activities in western Washington during 1984, a diplomatic as well as commercial coup for Washington State."[25] China's Ambassador to the U.S., Mr. Zhang Wenjin, came to Seattle to attend the opening celebrations at the invitation of the Pacific Science Center. At the Center's request, the Council coordinated the activities of Ambassador Zhang and his colleagues throughout the visit.

A very useful program that the Council also started in 1983 was called the Travel Support Program. It was made possible by a gift from Northwest Airlines. The support was later renewed by the airline every two years through the 1990s, in fact, through three more executive directors. By the summer of 1986, the Council had assisted more than forty Washingtonians to travel to China on cultural and educational projects. Grants took the form of reductions of international airfare and were made on a competitive basis. Recipients included teachers, researchers, writers, filmmakers, museum staff, artists, photographers, among others.

Of all the comings and goings that the Council oversaw, Chinese and American, ambassadors and governors, one of the highest-level stopovers in Washington state it received had to be the one by President Ronald Reagan on April 19, 1984. President Reagan was on his way to China to reciprocate the visit by then Chinese Premier Zhao Ziyang to the United States in January that year.

---

25. Washington State China Relations Council, *"Council News,"* Fall 1982

Accompanying President Reagan were Secretary of State George Shultz and Administrator of EPA William Ruckelshaus, a former Weyerhaeuser executive, among others. Escorting him through his 170-minute stay was Gov. John Spellman.[26]

The President was given a tour of the Port of Tacoma first that morning by George Weyerhaeuser, president and CEO of Weyerhaeuser Company, and was shown the company's China-bound logs and lumber. President Reagan then sat down for a group discussion on international trade at the headquarters of Weyerhaeuser Company in Federal Way, 25 miles south of downtown Seattle.

To see and hear the President that day were forty senior executives of the state's industrial, commercial, and agricultural sectors, many of them representing the Council member firms or organizations. Among them Edward E. Carlson, chairman emeritus of UAL Inc.; T.A Wilson, chairman and CEO of The Boeing Co.; Mary Gates, University of Washington regent; Tomio Moriguchi, president of Uwajimaya Inc.; Richard D. Ford, the Port of Seattle executive director; Richard D. Smith, the Port of Tacoma executive director; G. Robert Truex Jr., chairman and CEO of Rainier Bank; Nancy Jacob, dean of the UW Graduate School of Business Administration, and Richard J. Robbins, president of Robbins Co.[27]

Serving as the meeting chairman was the Council's Executive Director Kapp, who also had the honor to introduce President Reagan.

The President spoke first. He mentioned how the U.S. was China's third largest trading partner and the U.S. was China's leading foreign investor. He added that the U.S. had already signed a series of bilateral agreements with China covering trade and financial matters, and when he arrived in Beijing, he would continue the talks on agreements involving taxes and financial investment. He then said something that still rings true today:

> "There are other trade issues that we're still resolving with China, and I know that as in any relationship, there are going to be some growing pains. You know, as I do, that occasionally the interests of diplomacy and the interests of

---

26.   Richard Buck, "NW is first stop in Reagan's China visit," *The Seattle Times*, Apr. 19, 1984

27.   Ibid.

American industry sometimes seem to collide. Well, I see it as our job to reconcile the two and to make it easier for American businessmen to open up new markets on a fair footing."[28]

After President Reagan, Dr. George E. Taylor, president of Washington Council on International Trade made brief remarks and showed the group a slide show. Then J. K. Barrington, president of Washington State China Relations Council that year and senior vice president at First Interstate Bank of Washington, made a presentation on trade between Washington state and China. It was followed by a group discussion moderated by George Weyerhaeuser.

President Reagan listened to the group and also joined the discussion about the need for expanded trade with China and Japan. With full understanding of Washington state's dependence on exports, President Reagan told the state business leaders that he was definitely opposed to protectionism and would go to China as a salesman of American products.[29] He added, "I'll do everything I can up to the limit of not putting a 'Buy American' sticker on my bag."[30]

An archive photo by the Tacoma News-Tribune that day showed a seated President Reagan in the center of a group, tilting his head and looking at a standing Kapp. In the background was a banner reading in bold letters "Exports Mean Jobs."

Export or jobs were certainly important topics at Weyerhaeuser that day. What was at least equally important was President Reagan's stopover itself and his recognition of the Washington State China Relations Council. The visit brought the Council great publicity and visibility. It had to be a very encouraging experience for Kapp and the Council.

As if in celebration, something else encouraging soon followed. As Kapp wrote in the summer 1984 issue of the "Council News," "Council Membership Tops 100." Hitting the hundredth member mark was the Seattle law firm of Culp, Dwyer, Guterson & Grader.

---

28. Remarks During a Roundtable Discussion With Export Trade Industry Representatives in Tacoma, Washington, April 19, 1984, http://www.reagan.utexas.edu/archives/speeches/1984/41984b.htm
29. Neil Modie and Bruce Ramsay, "Reagan tells state business he'll be a 'salesman' in China," *Seattle Post-Intelligencer*, Apr. 19, 1984, p. A1
30. Ibid.

Early in 1985, Kapp happily announced another first for the Council: for the first time since its founding in 1979, the Council now had three people at work in its office. The new addition was Ms. Bao Lee-wah, as the new program assistant who spoke Mandarin, Shanghainese and Cantonese. Linda Eng, the administrative assistant, now became full time staffer. The Council also moved again, this time to Waterfront Place at 1011 Western Avenue, near both the Seattle waterfront and the heart of the city.[31] That year, serving as the Council president was William E. Franklin, group vice president-international at Weyerhaeuser Company.

In the summer of 1985, Kapp organized and led to China a group of twelve leading staffers of Washington State's U.S. senators and congressmen. In Beijing, as Kapp had arranged, the group had a series of meetings with leading Chinese figures in foreign affairs, foreign trade, international investment, and import and export. In Chengdu and Guangzhou, the group visited rural households, a tools plant, a port and a Sino-American joint venture in processed foods production. Members of the group expressed strong satisfaction upon returning. Kapp wrote in the newsletter that:

> "The Council's main purpose in assembling the mission, i.e., to assist the state's Congressional representatives in recognizing the implications for the state's China interests in their overall legislative responsibilities, seemed to be well realized."[32]

In mid October, with Council membership over 120[33], Kapp was pleased to announce the new make-up of the Council staff of three, this time with the Hong Kong-educated bilingual Mr. Kin Hung Luk as the new program associate. In a letter to Council members and directors, Kapp announced:

> "...Appointment of a full-time program associate, a major step forward in the Council's growth...With the addition of Kin Hung Luk to the staff, we believe that the Council will be able to strengthen existing services and add new ones."[34]

---

31. Washington State China Relations Council, *"Council News,"* Winter 1985
32. Washington State China Relations Council, *"Council News,"* Summer 1985
33. Washington State China Relations Council archives.
34. Washington State China Relations Council newsletter, Oct. 15, 1985

Kapp then listed a number of services that Mr. Luk would help to provide, such as languages services, member contact, and information searches.

In late October 1985, it was Governor Booth Gardner's turn to visit China with a delegation of state government officials, business leaders and the press. The governor and delegation visited Beijing, Shanghai and Chengdu, the capital of Sichuan. In Beijing they met then Chinese Vice Premier Li Peng as well as top officials from a number of Chinese government agencies from forestry to agriculture, from foreign affairs to friendship association. Council executive director Kapp was of course on the delegation. In fact, the winter 1986 Council newsletter contained a photo of Kapp shaking hands with Li Peng. Kapp, always the tallest in a group, was looking down at Li.

In Chengdu, Governor Gardner and the group visited a wood processing plant, an aircraft plant, a radio factory and an agricultural area. Members of the delegation also held discussions on further development of economic and cultural relations between Washington and Sichuan with their Sichuan counterparts.

Also in Chengdu, before a farewell banquet, Gov. Gardner acknowledged that he had earlier questioned the need to visit China, but now had no regrets. "To be successful here," he had realized, "you have to be willing to establish deep-seated personal relationships, and those relationships often precede commercial ones." He said he would continue to support strong relations with Sichuan Province.[35]

Back at SeaTac airport, Gov. Gardner told reporters that he and others on the Washington trade delegation had made substantial progress in stimulating investment in Washington and sales of Washington products, but it would be hard to measure the tangible results of the mission.[36] While the governor was being cautious, two tangible results were announced that day. One was from the spokesman of the state Department of Agriculture that a group of Washington farmers were ready to sign immediately a lucrative contract to sell grain seeds to China. Another was the expansion of academic relations between Chengdu University of Science and Technology and the University of Washington.[37]

---

35. Walter Hatch, "China mission to pay off in the long term, Gardner says," *The Seattle Times*, Oct. 23, 1985, p. B2
36. AP, "Gardner back with export trade plans," *The Seattle Times*, Oct. 25, 1985, p. C3
37. The Seattle Times, "China mission to pay off in the long term, Gardner says," Oct. 23, 1985

In early December 1985, the Council received a delegation from the China Science and Technology Exchange Center. STEC was subordinated to China's Scientific and Technical Commission, devoting itself primarily to the arrangement of technical exchanges between Chinese and foreign entities. Recognizing the importance of linking American actors with appropriate Chinese counterparts, the Council, represented by Kapp, and STEC, represented by Xia Yufu, signed a Memorandum of Understanding for a cooperative relationship. The Council also agreed to assist STEC in arranging visits to Washington state by STEC representatives and other Chinese technical specialists.[38]

In May 1986, the Council had the "distinct privilege," in Kapp's words, to plan and arrange for the visit to Seattle by another VIP from China, this time Vice Premier Yao Yilin and his delegation. Yao was second in ranking only to then Premier Zhao Ziyang and the highest-ranking visitor from China since Vice Premier Bo Yibo's visit in the fall of 1980. Seattle was Vice Premier Yao's last stop of a two-week trip to the U.S. that had included the annual meeting of the U.S.-China Joint Commission on Commerce and Trade in Washington D.C.

Arriving with Vice Premier Yao was Gan Ziyu, vice minister of China's State Planning Commission, Zhu Youlan, assistant to the minister of foreign economic relations and trade, Zhang Wenpu, head of American department of China's foreign ministry, and Han Xu, Chinese ambassador to the Untied States. They were here not for sightseeing, of course, but to look at Washington's airplane and high tech capabilities. The Council was ready to satisfy them.

After a red carpet greeting by Gov. Gardner, Mayor Royer and a number of other officials at Boeing Field, Mr. Yao and party were given a dinner by John M. Fluke, Jr., chairman and CEO of the John Fluke Manufacturing Company, a Council member.

Mr. Fluke was not just the head of his company, he also happened to be the president of the Council that year. At the dinner, Fluke told the guests about the Council and his views about America's need for two-way trade.

---

38.   Washington State China Relations Council, *"Council News,"* Winter 1986

In return, Vice Premier Yao acknowledged the Council's efforts and said, "I feel that we're old friends with each other although we've only met for the first time." [39]

Next day, Mr. Yao and the party visited a number of well-known Washington state trade entities "heavily involved with China," as Kapp said proudly, "all of them members of the Washington State China Relations Council."[40] They were The Boeing Company, the John Fluke Manufacturing Company, the Port of Seattle, The Robbins Company and Weyerhaeuser Company.

That night, Vice Premier Yao and party attended a state dinner in their honor given by Gov. Gardner, with 400 guests. In his remarks, Mr. Yao called Seattle a "shining pearl in this exuberant country,"[41] and said he believed that Washington could develop even closer ties to China. On what he called the greatest potential in the world for the United States and China to work as partners, Mr. Yao said:

> "The United States is the world's most developed country with enormous technical might. We are the largest developing country with abundant resources and a huge market. With our respective advantages, we can promote our common interests by cooperating together."[42]

For all the warm words and the success of Yao's visit, Gov. Gardner wrote in a letter to Kapp afterwards:

> "I am convinced that the visit of Vice Premier Yao Yilin was important to the trade and economic development agenda of the State of Washington. Your work in planning and making arrangements for the Vice Premier's activities while he was here was most effective and very helpful.

> "This letter is to thank you and China Relations Council for getting the Vice Premier to include our state in his itinerary and then doing such a good job for putting his time with us to such good use."[43]

---

39. Jack Swanson, "Chinese officials looking at state's high-tech potential," *Seattle Post-Intelligencer*, May 22, 1986, p A3
40. Washington State China Relations Council, *"Council News,"* Summer 1986
41. Jack Swanson, "Closer state ties with China foreseen," *Seattle Post-Intelligencer*, May 23, 1986, p. A3
42. Ibid.
43. Washington State Archives.

Wouldn't we all, as members and friends of the Council as well as all those individuals or organizations that have benefited from Washington State-China relations and Washington State-Sichuan relations want to say the same to Kapp, not just for Yao's visit, but for all of Kapp's superb service at the Council?

One person who gave high praise to Kapp and the Council for all of us was the U.S. Ambassador to China, Arthur W. Hummel, who was in town in early 1986 after completing his service in the People's Republic of China. As the featured speaker of the Council's sixth Annual Meeting at the Westin Hotel, Mr. Hummel said:

> "The Council is known throughout China, and is known to have a significant place in China-U.S. affairs." [44]

Kapp continued working as the executive director of the Council till mid-1987, having welcomed in Melvin M. Stewart, chairman of the board of Stevedoring Services of America, Inc., to be the Council president and seeing the Council membership reach 130.[45] Kapp had also set up a new membership structure that year with six categories—distinguished, sustaining, supporting, contributing, regular and associate.

Not just setting up the membership structure, Kapp had, over the seven years as its executive director, set the structure, tone and character of the Council, from its first banquet to first office, from its first newsletter to the first China trade conference, from receiving Chinese vice premiers to briefing an American president, from establishing Washington state relations with one Chinese province to establishing Council relations with organizations in various Chinese provinces. He was truly the Council's pioneer executive director and a giant in the Council history.

Kapp went on to "learn new skills and have new experiences," as he told me, by moving in 1987 to the Washington Council on International Trade (WCIT) as its president. After having worked in the China field for over 23 years since graduate school, his new job was a "vacation" from the China field, he said. But Kapp emphasized, "Presiding over WCIT opened new horizons for me and gave me a chance to learn about many subjects."

---

44. Washington State China Relations Council, "*Council News,*" Winter 1986
45. Washington State China Relations Council archives.

Yes, indeed. Kapp's new horizons were also much broader. They included his bringing the APEC Summit to Seattle in November 1993 almost single-handedly, accomplishing perhaps the biggest coup for Washington state as well as for himself. In fact, beginning in 1992, he had been serving concurrently as both president of WCIT and executive director of Washington State China Relations Council. A few months later, in the spring of 1994, Kapp left Seattle and the two local organizations he had served with distinction to take up the position of the president of a national organization: the US-China Business Council. Those of us remaining in Washington state were to watch Kapp operating and shining on the national stage of U.S.-China business relations in Washington D.C. for ten years to come, and with pride.

I am sure that Washingtonians were delighted in late 2004 when Kapp returned after over a decade in the other Washington. Making Washington state home once again in Port Townsend, Kapp now works as a consultant with major U.S. corporate clients pursuing business development in China. But as a renowned China specialist, reporters keep calling Kapp whenever China is in the news.

What did Kapp think, looking back, of his career switch from academe to non-profit business associations? I had to ask. Kapp's reply that came by email was what I had imagined it to be:

> "...For me, the non-academic life that opened up before me as the China Relations Council was born turned out to be far more rewarding...I found, in the ensuing 25 years, a great deal of stimulation, challenge, and enjoyment..."

Was China tiring him out yet? Kapp went on:

> "China remains challenging and profoundly interesting. Some aspects of working with China become routine over the years, but new and unfamiliar ones continue to emerge."

But this chapter wouldn't be complete without Kapp's current views on China after all these years, first as a China scholar, then as the executive director of the Council, and finally as a leading U.S.-China business advocate as well as China watcher. Was he generally optimistic or pessimistic towards China?

Like the professor he had once been, Kapp kindly and patiently listed for me a number of scholarly and other published works revolving around the theme of Westerners' expectations and hopes with respect to China and the degree to which such hopes turned out to be illusory or misguided. Then he wrote:

> "Having said all of that...you will find that my overall attitude toward engaging with China is one of respect but caution, and above all one of realistic recognition of many differences that continue to challenge Americans and Chinese when they seek to work jointly together."

Still I wouldn't let him go without asking for his comment on his own quote from early 1979, the one about the tremendously long road, the enormously complex challenge, the overwhelming transformation, the uncharted waters and the unclear ramifications that China had been facing. Kapp responded this way, with his trademark realism:

> "Nothing to back away from there; Twenty six years later, perhaps those 'ramifications' are somewhat clearer than they were in 1979. But who could deny that the history of the past quarter-century has basically validated the comments you quote?"

I had no more questions.

Robert A. Kapp, 2005

2.2

William Abnett—Through Tragic Times
(Executive Director 1987–1992)

William B. Abnett, around 1988

If there is anyone among the founders and directors of the Washington State China Relations Council that makes this writing a bit heavy, it is Mr. William B. Abnett.

It was during Mr. Abnett's tenure as the executive director that army tanks crushed the Tiananmen demonstration in Beijing, sending the Council as well as U.S.-China relations to their lowest point. That was in 1989. One year later, Abnett's personal life was crushed, too, with his wife, the love of his life, lost to brain cancer. If the Tiananmen tragedy almost killed the Council, as Abnett commented once, the death of his wife almost killed him.

I arrived in Seattle from Shenzhen, China in May 1989 and learned about the Washington State China Relations Council soon after. Sometime in the middle of that year, a friend and I visited Abnett in his office at the Council. At that time, the Council had already moved to a new location in the Fourth & Vine Building on Fourth Avenue.

Before taking the job as the executive director of the Council in 1987, I had learned, Abnett had served as the director for Chinese affairs in the office of the United States Trade Representative (USTR) at the Reagan White House. Responsible for developing and coordinating the administration's trade policy toward China, Abnett had participated in all bilateral and multilateral trade negotiations involving U.S. and China, including steel and textiles and several rounds in 1986 on China's entry, or re-entry, into the General Agreement on Tariffs and Trade (GATT), the predecessor of the World Trade Organization (WTO).

From 1982 to 1985, Abnett had worked in Beijing, serving as chief of the economic affairs section at the American Embassy. We saw proof of that on his desk that day: a big porcelain cup with the Chinese characters for "Beijing Yogurt Company" on it. It was being used as a penholder.

Abnett was friendly and professional, or diplomatic. If Tiananmen was heavy on his mind, he didn't show. But I did read in a local paper later that after the June 4th crackdown in Beijing, Abnett, an enthusiastic hiker, went to Mt. Rainier and camped overnight to vent, or absorb, the shock and frustration. My friend and I, however, were not there that day to talk about China. The visit was about some translation work for a member company doing business in China. But that was the start of my interest in the Council.

Born in 1949, coincidentally the year of the founding of the People's Republic of China, Abnett grew up in Philadelphia and earned his bachelor's in government from Franklin and Marshall College in Lancaster, Penn. in 1971. It was there Abnett took his first Chinese language lessons from a Beijing-born Chinese-American teacher. When did Abnett first become interested in China? I asked him years later when we met again. He said it was at ten, when a teacher talked about Mao in class one day. That would have been 1959. I wondered if the teacher had been telling the class about Mao's failed Great Leap Forward.

After college, Abnett came to Seattle to do graduate work in Chinese studies at the University of Washington, with a scholarship. After earning his master's in East Asian Studies in 1973, Abnett went on to serve at a number of government posts, including military and diplomatic, from Vietnam to Hong Kong to Beijing. In Vietnam, Abnett was a company commander, directing 400 linguists from a number of bases.[46] That made Abnett the second veteran among the Council founders and directors after Mr. Richard Kirk.

Before starting at the Council in July 1987, Abnett had been working for the USTR. In fact, when the media first learned in April that year he was being considered for the position, Abnett was stopping over in Seattle on his way back to Washington, D.C., after a round of trade talks in Beijing.

Why did Abnett leave USTR for Seattle? One reason, as Abnett told a local paper, was the pace in Washington, D.C. The 18-hour days and seven-day weeks all but excluded a family life. The second was the Northwest's lifestyle and the wilderness.[47] The third, as Abnett added: "I look at this as returning home…I guess the important thing is this job opened up, combining China and trade, in a refreshingly wonderful free-trade state."[48]

Whatever the reasons, Abnett's impressive credentials in Chinese trade and economic affairs in the Reagan Administration made some describe his hiring as a coup. The more practical side of his appointment was, however, well expressed by the Council president Melvin Stewart, chairman of Stevedoring Services of America: "Abnett's knowledge of China trade should be a big boost to Washington businesses seeking greater access to the China market."[49]

U.S.-China business relations were at a high point at the time of Abnett's arrival, with a peak period for Washington log exports to China, expanded service by Cosco (China Ocean Shipping Co.) at the Port of Seattle, and talks about a

---

46. Steve Wilhelm, "Bill Abnett takes the China crisis personally," *Puget Sound Business Journal*, Jun. 11, 1990, p. 1

47. Ibid.

48. Evelyn Iritani, "China Expert Is 'Coming Home' To A New Job", *Seattle Post-Intelligencer*, Jun. 27, 1987, p. B6

49. Ibid.

Chinese-Boeing joint venture to build airplanes. Things were so upbeat that Abnett was told by the Council's board to focus strictly on trade promotion.[50]

Focusing on trade promotion was Abnett's forte and exactly what he was going to do. Trade promotion was also to define Abnett's directorship over the next five years or so. And trade issues were waiting for him.

In the summer of 1987, an Omnibus Trade Bill was before Congress. It contained everything from relaxation of export controls to retaliation against trading partners with large surpluses. Major exporters in Washington, such as The Boeing Company and ITT Rayonier, believed the bill was protectionist and needed to be blocked.

Earlier that year, the Council's executive committee had decided for the first time that it was lawful for the Council to lobby Congress, if necessary, to accomplish the Council's mission.[51] The decision had been made just in time.

In answering to the call of the Council as well as the business community, and along with Seattle's other major players in international trade including the Greater Seattle Chamber of Commerce and the Washington Council on International Trade, Abnett made efforts against the elements in the bill that would hurt the trade of Washington state.

In an interview with a local paper, Abnett said that he was focusing his efforts on opposing an amendment by Rep. John Heinz, R-Pa., which would force China to artificially raise its prices to a level comparable to the largest-volume market economy supplier or risk anti-dumping penalties. He said that would penalize China for its low-wage competitive advantage and would badly hurt the country's efforts to break into world markets."[52]

Abnett's and others' efforts must have worked. The bill did not become law. It was not until the summer of 1988 that a revised and compromised bill named the

---

50. Steve Wilhelm, "Bill Abnett takes the China crisis personally," *Puget Sound Business Journal*, Jun. 11, 1990

51. Washington State China Relations Council archives.

52. Evelyn Iritani, "Trade Bill Frustrate Lawmakers Wrangling May Delay Votes Until Next Year," *Seattle Post-Intelligencer*, Oct. 16, 1987, p. B4

"Omnibus Trade and Competitiveness Act" would be passed by Congress and signed by President Reagan.

In November 1987, at the invitation of the U.S. Senate China Trade Caucus, Abnett chaired a panel and joined another at the first U.S. Senate China Trade Caucus Symposium, to the pride of the Council.

With the arrival of January 1988 came an exceptional result of the Council's trade promotion and assistance work: a Bellevue developer, MGM Development Co., landed a large deal in China to develop an industrial park in a special economic zone in Tianjin, China's third-largest port and one of the fastest-growing industrial areas. Abnett was very pleased. He described the project as unprecedented. Tianjin Mayor Li Ruihuan, Abnett told the press, was spearheading one of China's most progressive economic programs. Combining Tianjin's political clout and MGM Inc.'s development expertise was a remarkable feat.[53]

In February, Abnett invited Chinese Ambassador Mr. Han Xu to Seattle to speak to the Council's annual membership meeting. Ambassador Han advised that Washington traders should concentrate on providing advanced production technology and equipment, work on relaxing U.S. export controls towards China, get involved in joint ventures to combine Western know-how with cheap Chinese labor, and work against protectionist legislation that would hurt China's ability to export to America and, in turn, limit the country's ability to buy Boeing airplanes and Northwest lumber and grain.[54]

With the death of Taiwan President Jiang Jingguo a month earlier, Ambassador Han also talked about relations between the mainland and Taiwan. It was no easy matter, as Abnett had found out, in a state like Washington that was trading in millions with both sides of the Taiwan Strait. Back in September 1987, Governor Booth Gardner had to be briefed by the U.S. government, the Chinese government, the Taiwan office in the U.S. as well as Abnett in dealing with Taiwan and addressing Taiwan properly at a banquet attended by Taiwan officials without violating America's "one-China" policy.

---

53.   Evelyn Iritani, "Bellevue Firm Lands Big China Project," *Seattle Post-Intelligencer*, Jan. 22, 1988, p. A1

54.   Evelyn Iritani, "The Two Chinas Close The Gap A Little—In Downtown Seattle," *Seattle Post-Intelligencer*, Feb. 2, 1988, p. A2

In April, to his great delight, Abnett had his former boss, U.S. Trade Representative Clayton Yeutter, in town to speak at a breakfast meeting sponsored by the Council.

Ambassador Yeutter talked about the trade bill, the stock market, the trade deficit, Taiwan, and, of course, China. Asked if the U.S. government would reconsider its categorization of China as communist when setting trade policies, Yeutter said he did not think China had liberalized its economy enough to be considered a full-fledged free trader.[55] In the same breath, however, Yeutter also commented how the economic and social changes taking place in China were "mind-boggling," and how the country's economic reform, "may sound like socialism, but walks like capitalism."[56]

That's what Abnett believed also. He wholeheartedly went about promoting trade with China during the remainder of 1988. In May, the Council co-sponsored a "Meet China's Top CEOs!" conference in Seattle. In June, Abnett joined 900 American executives at the U.S./China Joint Session on Industry, Trade and Economic Development conference in Beijing, and participated in two panel discussions on copyright protection and intellectual property protection in China. Also on that trip, Abnett and program associate Kin Hung Luk met in Chengdu with the newly appointed Sichuan Governor, Zhang Haoruo, and discussed improving commercial aspects of the friendly relationship. Late that year, Abnett was back in the nation's capital again at the invitation of Secretary of State George Shultz to attend the signing ceremony of the new U.S.-China maritime treaty.

Toward the end of 1988, joining the discussion among Washington state businesses about trade prospects in the year to come, especially amidst the talk of the Chinese government's efforts to curtail major capital spending projects, Abnett said with confidence that he didn't expect the Chinese government's campaign to cool its domestic economy to have a lasting impact on trade with this region. He predicted provincial authorities would continue to buy logs and

---

55.   Evelyn Iritani, "Yeutter To Taiwan: 'Go Jump In Lake' US Trade Representative Tells State Not To Fear Diplomatic Arm Twisting," *Seattle Post-Intelligencer*, Apr. 16, 1988, p. B3

56.   Ibid.

other Northwest products regardless of edicts from Beijing, because "the center can no longer call the shots."[57]

Abnett was optimistic for a reason. As stated in the annual report by Mr. Richard H. Harding, president of the Council that year and senior vice president of First Interstate Bank, "While 1988 was a banner year in overall U.S.-China relations, it was also a record-breaking year in trade between Washington state and the People's Republic of China." The total two-way trade had increased to $2 billion, up from $1.4 billion the previous year,[58] making Washington state China's largest American trading partner.

Still, there was something to worry about, something that seemed to become the theme of Abnett's work at the Council: China's Most Favored Nation (MFN) trade status. Before the year closed, Abnett urged representatives of the incoming Bush administration to encourage China's market reforms by giving it the MFN status that would allow it to sell goods more competitively in the United States. As he said, "I think it's great to have the Chinese playing by international trade rules."[59]

It was with the hope that China could play by international rules with continued MFN that Abnett started the year of 1989. In the first issue of his new quarterly newsletter "Insider," he wrote in the "Notes from the Executive Director":

> "Our newsletter differs from other China newsletters in that ours consists primarily of excerpts by Council members about their organizations' particular involvement with China. The purpose of the newsletter is to disseminate to our members practical information and tips that are valuable to those colleagues doing business with China."[60]

In it, Abnett also urged members to complete an enclosed questionnaire and return it to the Council's commerce committee as soon as possible. The commerce committee was an umbrella organization Abnett had created to coordinate the Council's seven sectoral groups: forest products, transportation, manufactur-

---

57. Evelyn Iritani, "Trade Winds Are Calm," *Seattle Post-Intelligencer*, Apr. Dec. 29, 1988, p. B6
58. Ibid.
59. Ibid.
60. Washington State China Relations Council, *"Insider,"* Spring, 1989

ing, export assistance, finance, travel, and law and business. The committee was compiling a Washington State China Relations Council trade directory for distribution in China.

Even though the newsletter also included a brief titled "Hu's Death Touched off Student Demonstrations" by the Council program associate Kin Hung Luk, no one at the time could ever have imagined what was to happen in Tiananmen Square.

During May, the political upheaval in China had prompted many U.S. companies to postpone visits or evacuate some staff and dependents until the crisis eased. Abnett, watching Beijing closely, said he knew of no Washington companies that had withdrawn staff.[61]

Things changed fast, however. With tanks rolling into Tiananmen Square and troops opening fire on unarmed demonstrators on June 4, 1989, the world reacted with rage and disbelief. Abnett immediately joined many in Congress, liberals and conservatives, in demanding President Bush take a stronger stand on China by ending military aid:

> "Bush has a moral obligation to say something stronger…There is a huge difference between one billion people and a bunch of old octogenarians clinging to power…This is an outrage."[62]

It was. It was also personal. Abnett learned that even the diplomatic apartment building along Beijing's main avenue where he had lived for three years were showered with bullets during the crackdown.

That was when, I assume, Abnett packed up and went to Mt. Rainier…

But when Abnett returned from the mountains, he did so with a conclusion: ending trade would hurt only the Chinese people, whose lives had been improved by China's economic openness.[63]

---

61.   PI-Staff and News Services, "Business In China On Hold A Time Of Hand-Wringing For American Companies," *Seattle Post-Intelligencer*, May 24, 1989

62.   PI-Staff and News Services, "End Arms Aid To China, Top Lawmakers Insist," *Seattle Post-Intelligencer*, Jun. 5, 1989, p. A5

63.   Sylvia Wieland Nogaki, "China-trade council tackles dilemmas posed by Tiananmen," *The Seattle Times*, May 14, 1990

Abnett plunged back into work, busily arranging and hosting a series of special Council programs on the political, economic, and historical implications of Tiananmen. One of the programs was poignantly titled, "Whither China?"[64]

At the same time, Abnett kept his "Insider" watch on China, which was typical of Abnett with his connections in the State Department, USTR and other federal agencies. In the summer 1989 issue of the newsletter, Abnett informed the members of the latest development toward China in Washington D.C.:

> "A well-placed source said that Secretary of State Baker was the strongest proponent in the Bush Administration of imposing economic sanctions against China. According to this source, Commerce Secretary Mosbacher opposed Baker and won the support of President Bush. Reportedly, USTR Carla Hills sided with Mosbacher." [65]

That was good news for the Council. But still some in Congress were calling for taking away China's MFN. Abnett formed an alliance with his predecessor Robert Kapp, now president of WCIT (Washington Council on International Trade). Together they expressed to the media their opposition to economic sanctions against China. They believed that a total break in economic relations would undermine U.S. influence in China and encourage the Communist government to retreat from the world. The result, they said, would be fewer opportunities for Chinese people to study and travel overseas and fewer chances for U.S. companies to do business.[66] Abnett added:

> "Now, more than ever, we need people-to-people relations, cultural relations, educational relations, so the light won't go out. It would be a travesty, a tragedy, if all of a sudden we were to sever relations."[67]

It was in the same spirit that Washington State had retained its sister-state relationship with Sichuan Province, as had Seattle with Chongqing, even though

---

64. Washington State China Relations Council archives.
65. Washington State China Relations Council, "*Insider*," Summer 1989
66. Evelyn Iritani, "How Far Can We Go In Punishing Foreign Leaders," *Seattle Post-Intelligencer*, Jun. 26, 1989, p. A1
67. Ibid.

San Francisco had severed ties with its Chinese sister city Shanghai, following the Tiananmen crackdown.

Nevertheless, it was a time of frustration and confusion. On one hand, a Redmond based textile importer couldn't receive on time its $1 million cotton apparel order from China because of the post Tiananmen chaos.[68] On the other, MGM Inc., the Bellevue developer, had finally signed the $17 million contract for the large industrial complex in Tianjin.[69] Both companies got words of caution from Abnett. To the importer, Abnett suggested that it would be prudent to protect itself by looking for alternative sources in the short term. To the developer, Abnett suggested that they should push for more concessions from the Chinese by including in the contract clauses for a share of the Chinese domestic market and repatriation of foreign currency. Yet, at the same time, Abnett's frustration with the whole China situation showed:

> "As others have said, how can you believe anything that's written in a contract by people who are lying to you about Tiananmen Square?"[70]

How exactly? With the topic of "Doing Business with Post-Tiananmen China," Abnett presided over the Council's seventh annual China Trade Update conference in late November, continuing the tradition Kapp had started in 1983. Abnett had his friend from his State Department days, Douglas H. Paal, as the keynote speaker. Paal was the senior director for Asian affairs on the National Security Council and President Bush's chief China advisor. Among other things, Mr. Paal told the audience that President Bush had suggested that both the United States and China should act together to end the deadlock in the bilateral relationship. Other speakers included Zheng Wanzhen, Chinese consul general in San Francisco; George Lee, a former economics officer with the U.S. embassy in Beijing and director of the U.S.-China Business Institute at San Francisco State University; and State Department China economics specialist William Primosch.[71]

---

68. Ron Redmond, "The China Connection Is Frayed Textile Importers Say Political Upheavals Have Made Trade Unreliable," *Seattle Post-Intelligencer*, Jul. 17, 1989

69. Ron Redmond, "Bellevue Company Signs Development Deal With China," *Seattle Post-Intelligencer*, Aug. 10, 1989, p. A1

70. Ibid.

71. Ron Redmond, "China Won't Ditch Communism, Diplomat Insists," *Seattle Post-Intelligencer*, Nov. 30, 1989, p. A4

In the fall issue of "Insider," Abnett explained to the members the two trips to China by then National Security Advisor Brent Scowcroft and Deputy Secretary State Lawrence S. Eagleburger after Tiananmen:

> "President Bush has said that the purpose of the July visit was to express high-level criticism of the crackdown directly to the Chinese leadership, instead of going through diplomatic channels. The White House reported that the goal of the second Scowcroft-Eagleburger trip was to break 'some of the ice between us.'" [72]

But breaking the ice was easier said than done. With the ice far from being broken, there came in the cold December of 1989 perhaps the biggest dilemma for Washington state's business and community leaders, and the Council: the Chinese wanted to hold a large-scale trade conference in Seattle in the following April to be attended by possibly as many as 500 Chinese, the largest delegation ever from China to the U.S. [73]

The Chinese party making the proposal was the Chinese Association of Science and Technology, the Chinese organizer of the U.S./China Joint Session on Industry, Trade and Economic Development in Beijing back in June 1988. They had first approached Norm Swanson, chairman of the Spokane-based Citizen Ambassador Program, the co-organizer of the Beijing meeting. The conference was to be the third of the Beijing events. Not only the conference, the Chinese also offered to make Washington state the hub of their trade activities in the U.S. with a permanent trade exhibition center in Seattle, possibly with consulate-level functions, to seek landing rights in Seattle for China's international airlines, and to set up a management program at the University of Washington.

The dilemma: on one side was the continuing outrage on the part of the Washingtonians over the Tiananmen crackdown; on the other, the desire to maintain the existing ties between Washington state and China. Abnett expressed it this way:

> "My gut response is this is a great opportunity, don't lose it. But on the other hand, if the wrong combination of events occur—if the American people and

---

72. Washington State China Relations Council, *"Insider,"* Fall 1989
73. Ron Redmond, "China Woos State As Trade Hub But Proposal For Seattle Meeting Poses A Dilemma," *Seattle Post-Intelligencer*, Jan. 5, 1990, p. A1

congress get so upset with China and China continues its crackdown—it could be a bad thing and it could all collapse."[74]

A meeting was thus held among three gentlemen, Swanson, Abnett, and Ralph Munroe, the state's Secretary of State. After their meeting, the three called a larger meeting attended by representatives of prominent local businesses and organizations involved in trade and other ties with China, including The Boeing Co., Weyerhaeuser Co. and John Fluke Manufacturing Co.

Why Seattle, the attendees asked? According to Swanson, the Chinese had had two other possible choices, California and New York. They chose Seattle, Washington, because the state had been more moderate in its criticism of the Chinese government and had not abrogated its sister-state and sister-city relationships.

Was the Chinese request a sincere gesture to improve damaged bilateral relations or a ploy to use Washington state to repair its tarnished image? With the uncertainty of China's political and economic future, with Congress pressing economic sanctions against China and the opposition of the public to renew China ties, the group decided to tell the Chinese it would be best to postpone the conference until September, after the Goodwill Games scheduled for July 1990.[75] To that suggestion, the Chinese reluctantly agreed later.

All this happened while John M. Swihart, vice president of The Boeing Company, served as president of the Council. He accurately recorded the difficulty the Council faced in the annual report,

> "...year (1989) began on a highly auspicious note: the United States and China had just finished celebrating the tenth anniversary of the establishment of diplomatic relations between our two countries. We in the China Relations Council looked forward to 1989 as the year in which two ten-year milestones with great significance to Washington state would be attained. First would be the ten-year anniversary of the docking of the Liu Lin Hai—the first vessel from the People's Republic of China to call at an American port since 1949. And later, in August, we would celebrate the Council's tenth birthday.

> Our plans for a festive ten-year anniversary were disrupted, however, by the tragic events of June 4 in Beijing. The China Relations Council deplores the

---

74.   Ibid.
75.   Ibid.

Chinese Government's brutality in using military force to suppress the unarmed demonstrators, but at the same time opposes the imposition by the U.S. Government of economic sanctions against China…"[76]

Mr. Swihart went on to reiterate the Council's mission: to improve and expand economic and cultural trade ties between Washington state and China, and the Council's belief that any efforts by our government to enact measures to restrict those ties would only serve to harm the Chinese people. He ended the report this way:

"What we need now is more—not less—contact with China. The most important lesson that we have learned from the events of Tiananmen is that the mission of Washington State China Relations Council is more important now than at any time in our ten-year history."[77]

That was a historic and moving statement. One could only imagine how hard it must have been for every one of the Council, from the president to the executive director, from members of the board to member firms, to mark the Council's tenth birthday with the tragedy of Tiananmen and to see the Council membership fall to 104, from a high of 130 in 1986.[78]

When news came in early January 1990 of Beijing's lifting of martial law, some dismissed it as an empty gesture. But Abnett saw differently: "It's more than symbolic because the Chinese leadership was terrified of easing up after what happened in Romania and Eastern Europe. By lifting martial law, they're taking a big risk."[79]

However, Abnett also believed that China must take further steps toward easing strained relations with the U.S. before state government and business leaders could make a final decision on whether to sponsor a Seattle conference. That was not just Abnett's view, it was also the Council's view.

The Council was ready to make that view known in a more formal setting. On Jan. 19, 1990, at the Council's annual membership meeting in the Westin Hotel,

---

76.   Washington State China Relations Council archives.
77.   Ibid.
78.   Ibid.
79.   Ron Redmond, "China's Lifting Of Martial Law Significant Says State Expert," *Seattle Post-Intelligencer*, Jan. 11, 1990, p. A9

Abnett had invited Mr. Zhao Xixin, minister of the PRC embassy in Washington D.C., to be the guest speaker. With a group of anti-Chinese demonstrators in the street below, Ambassador Zhao expressed his support for all of Beijing's proposals to the state and said Washington state could play a lead role in restoring strained Sino-U.S. relations by agreeing to sponsor the trade conference. The Council members, however, took the opportunity to suggest that Beijing should allow dissident Fang Lizhi to safely leave his sanctuary in the U.S. embassy, release political prisoners, and issue some sort of statement expressing regret for the loss of life last June.[80]

Although without indication of a statement of regret from Beijing, Ambassador Zhao did inform of the members of a possible compromise on the issue of Fang Lizhi and a series of "important and positive steps" that China had taken, such as Beijing's acceptance of a new VOA correspondent, the agreement to resume the Fulbright scholars program, the acceptance of 20 American teachers in Sichuan Province, among others.[81] With these, plus the end of martial law in Beijing and the release of more than five hundred people arrested for their part in the Tiananmen demonstration, the Council's view grew more positive.

It was with that view that Abnett got ready in late February to lead a 16-member group of Washingtonians to China. The group included Secretary of State Ralph Munroe, who was also traveling as part of a Secretaries of State Association group, Norman Swanson, head of the Citizen Ambassador Program of People-to-People Inc., as well as representatives from the Port of Seattle, Seattle Trade Center, Seattle's Chongqing Sister City Association, the University of Washington, and Weyerhaeuser.[82] The delegation was hosted by the Chinese Association of Science and Technology. The purpose of the meeting was to lay out the details for the proposed conference.

Distancing itself from the group, however, the state Department of Trade and Economic Development had issued a statement earlier, saying that it was not planning to recognize or endorse the conference in the current environment of U.S.-China relations.

---

80. Ron Redmond, "Chinese See Key Role For State Diplomat Spells Out Conditions," *Seattle Post-Intelligencer*, Jan. 19, 1990, p. A2
81. Ibid.
82. Washington State Archives.

Responding to the statement and the critics contending that the delegation would become a party to the communist government's campaign to buy respectability in the aftermath of Tiananmen, the delegation said that it intended to express its disgust over the massacre and would avoid being used by the Chinese propaganda machine.[83]

As the co-organizer/leader of the delegation, Abnett said his key goals on the trip would be to spell out to the Chinese the conditions for holding a successful trade conference and to explore the sincerity of the Chinese proposal to make Seattle a trade hub.[84]

But the controversy wouldn't die. As the Washington delegation attended the welcoming banquet in the Great Hall of the People, a cartoon appeared in Seattle Post-Intelligencer depicting the delegation toasting with their Chinese hosts. One delegate in the cartoon was saying, "Banquets! Luxurious hotels! All expenses paid! These Chinese may not know how to treat their citizens…" Another delegate was reading from a fortune cookie, "You would sell your mother for an export deal." The hands of the waiter in the picture were chained.[85]

That cartoon hurt Abnett deeply, and for many years to come. The artist and readers may have known about the trip, but they probably did not know that in Beijing while the two sides agreed to stage the trade conference in Seattle in October, Abnett stated bluntly to the Chinese that the conference would be scrapped if there were further bloodshed in China.[86] They also probably did not hear what Abnett said, as he strongly believed, that despite their anger over Tiananmen, "Most Americans don't want China to return to the Maoist era of fanatical Red Guards. We fought with them in Korea. We don't want to do that again…There is much more to be gained for China and the U.S. by keeping the door open than by closing it."[87] They certainly did not learn that when Abnett arrived home in Seattle from that trip, the house was empty. His wife had been taken to an emergency room.

---

83. Ibid.
84. Tom Brown, "Trip to China to Test Relations," *The Seattle Times*, Feb. 25, 1990.
85. David Horsey, *Seattle Post-Intelligencer*, Mar. 2, 1990
86. Tom Brown, Sylvia Wieland Nogaki, "Trade Meet With China Here In Oct.," *The Seattle Times*, Feb. 27, 1990.
87. Tom Brown, "Tension Underlies Trade Group's Visit—U.S. Memories of Massacre Tinge Meeting," *The Seattle Times*, Mar. 1, 1990

Back in office, however, Abnett continued doing what he believed to be right. The annual battle in Congress over China's MFN was coming up again. The prospect was not good, a year after Tiananmen.

In May, Abnett again had Douglas Paal, director of Asian affairs on the National Security Council, speaking to a Council luncheon. According to Mr. Paal, President Bush did not want to fight Congress over MFN without the active support of the American business community and those Americans with an interest in maintaining good U.S.-China relations.

Therefore, in the spring issue of the "Insider" newsletter, Abnett presented the Council members with a detailed MFN timetable, from the June 3 deadline for submission of the presidential waiver to extend China's MFN to the June-August House and Senate action, including hearings and a joint resolution. He urged members to take action:

> "Unless American business and public opinion weigh in heavily to support renewal of China's MFN, there is a good chance that Congress will vote against China this summer. Because the stakes are so high—loss of MFN could mean loss of U.S.-China trade—and the MFN issue goes to the very quick of the Washington State China Relations Council, we urge all of our members and directors aggressively to lobby Congress, in all-out effort to prevent China's MFN treatment from being rescinded."[88]

With MFN, which had been granted to China soon after the normalization of relations in 1979, two-way trade between the U.S. and China had grown from $1.1 billion prior to 1979 to $18 billion in 1989, in spite of the fallout from Tiananmen. Of the total, Washington state alone accounted for about $2.6 billion,[89] with between 20,000 to 24,000 jobs linked to it, as estimated by Abnett in 1990.

Without MFN, as a local paper reported, "Boeing could lose several billion dollars in airliner sales over the next few years. ITT Rayonier and Weyerhaeuser

---

88. Washington State China Relations Council, "*Insider*," Spring, 1990
89. Tom Brown, "Will China Keep Favored Trade Status," *The Seattle Times*, May 13, 1990

could lose part of their wood-products markets. The cost of Barbie dolls, G.I. Joes and popular Nike Air sports shoes could skyrocket."[90]

Abnett knew the stakes. He wrote a letter to the members of the state congressional delegation, stating, "Washington state has been the leading beneficiary of strong trade ties between the U.S. and China…Many of our companies, big and small, have opened offices in China…" [91] Not only that, a number of Chinese companies had also been setting up shop in Washington state, doing business ranging from steamship, fishing, timber, import-export, aircraft to real estate.[92]

On May 24, 1990, to the relief of the Council and local businesses, President Bush extended MFN to China for another year. Defending his decision, Bush said, "It's not a favor we're doing. This decision is the proper decision and it has nothing to do with saying we're condoning human rights excesses."[93] But the opponents in Congress could still block the extension with a resolution of disapproval. And they were ready to do so.

Abnett was ready, too, ready to testify before Congress on China's MFN. On June 21, 1990, Abnett was among a number of witnesses at the hearings titled "U.S.-People's Republic of China Trade Relations (PRC), Including Most-Favored-Nation Trade Status for the PRC" before the Subcommittee on Trade of the House Committee on Ways and Means.

After informing the panel of the mission of the Washington State China Relations Council and predicting disastrous effects on U.S.-China trade, Abnett commented on the dire political consequences of removing MFN from China,

> "First, bilateral political relations would deteriorate, perhaps irreparably. Inside China, hardliners in the leadership would be strengthened—not weakened…Second, it would victimize the victims—the ordinary people of China, who are the very individuals that the American government is striving to protect…Finally…In 1989, fully 70 percent of American imports from China were transshipped through Hong Kong for value-added processing…With the

---

90. Ibid.
91. Ibid.
92. Sylvia Wieland Nogaki, "The China Connection—Mainland Companies Set Up Businesses in Seattle Area," *The Seattle Times*, May 5, 1990
93. Staff, "China Gets Trade Break—Bush's Controversial Decision Benefits State," *The Seattle Times*, May 24, 1990

1997 question looming so large in the minds of Hong Kong people, shouldn't the U.S. Congress be supporting rather than undermining the Hong Kong economy?"[94]

Abnett ended his testimony with a formal plea:

"The Washington State China Relations Council hopes that the U.S. Congress will vote to extend MFN trade status for the People's Republic of China for another year."[95]

Not just testifying in Congress, Abnett also visited the Chinese Embassy and had lunch with the Chinese Ambassador Zhu Qizhen. Having known Zhu before, Abnett took the opportunity to ask questions, including measures the Chinese government could take to improve the relationship. He gave it his best shot in Washington, D.C.

Back in Washington state, however, an unfortunate dispute came up in August between Abnett and Swanson, the organizer of the proposed Chinese conference. Believing that Congress' decision on China's MFN wouldn't come until around Labor Day, Abnett had suggested the conference be held in spring 1991. Swanson, however, insisted on holding the event from Nov. 28 to Dec.1, gambling that Congress would not scuttle China's MFN. After a board meeting and vote, Abnett informed Swanson that the Council could not support the conference because of the uncertainty over China's MFN and inadequate time to plan the conference if the status was renewed.[96] The State, the City of Seattle, and even The Boeing Company, also declined to endorse the conference.

It must have been a painful decision to make on the part of the Council with its focus on promoting trade between Washington state and China. It must also have been a painful announcement to make on the part of Abnett who had

---

94. Hearings Before the Subcommittee on Trade of the Committee on Ways And Means House of Representatives, One Hundred First Congress, Second Session, June 19 and 21, 1990, Serial 101–107, U.S Government Printing Office, Washington: 1990, p. 358–368

95. Ibid.

96. Tom Brown, "China Trade Conference Loses Support," *The Seattle Times*, Aug. 9, 1990

endured criticism and caricature working to make sure the conference would be a success.

But more pain was waiting for Abnett. Toward the end of September 1990, his wife Susan, who had been battling cancer for several years, died. His pain was obvious in an earlier interview with a local paper, "With your wife ailing and the whole China thing falling apart, you have to ask yourself if it's worth doing this."[97]

Three weeks later, in late October, China's MFN became firm for another year. Was Abnett celebrating?

Late November came. The Chinese arrived, 370 of them, including 100 officials, 250 representatives of 100 exhibiting companies and 20 staff of the Chinese Association for Science and Technology, the Chinese organizer.[98] The "U.S.-China Symposium and Exposition on Industry, Technology, Trade and Economic Cooperation" opened as scheduled in the Seattle International Trade Center. According to Roger Collis of Pacifica Foundation, hired by Swanson to organize the event, about 175 Americans, most representing small firms, had signed up for the conference and planned to talk to the 100 Chinese companies.[99] Still, it was "Little Fanfare for Largest U.S.-China Trade Conference," as described in the headline of a local paper, except perhaps for the presence of James Lilley, U.S. ambassador to China, and Zhu Qizhen, Chinese ambassador to the U.S., at the final session of the conference.

Abnett was not invited to the conference. But at the suggestion of Kapp, president of WCIT, Abnett, representing the Council, did join Kapp and the state's Department of Trade and Economic Development in hosting an independent reception for about 100 of the Chinese visitors. It was meant to "take some of the chill off the local response," in Kapp's words.[100]

---

97. Steve Wilhelm, "Bill Abnett takes China crisis personally," *Puget Sound Business Journal,* Jun. 11, 1990

98. Tom Brown, "Prospects—Talking Trade Amid Tensions—370 Chinese Visiting Seattle For Exhibition, Symposium," *The Seattle Times,* Nov. 25, 1990

99. Charles Dunshire, "Little Fanfare For Largest U.S.-China Trade Conference," *Seattle Post-Intelligencer,* Nov. 29, 1990

100. Ibid.

In the 1990 annual report, Mr. Timothy C. Herlich, the Council president and district sales manager of Northwest Airlines, wrote:

> "Nineteen-hundred-and-ninety was by far the most seriously strained year in U.S.-China relations since both countries established diplomatic relations over a decade ago. It was also the most challenging year in the Council's 11-year history...
>
> "Enhancing commercial and cultural trade ties with China is a long-term proposition; we must anticipate peaks and valleys, ebbs and flows. We must keep the Council going..." [101]

Yes, to keep it going, Abnett pressed on. There was good reason to do so, too. Despite the chill in the Seattle winter of 1990, Washington state's trade with China that year reached $3 billion, again more than any other state.[102]

1991 was another busy year for Abnett, which included organizing the Council luncheons with Washington's congressional delegation for China's MFN, meeting with the Seattle representative of Taiwan's Coordination Council for North American Affairs to explore new opportunities for Washington businesses,[103] receiving a high-level Chinese purchasing delegation spending $1 billion on U.S. goods, including Boeing airplanes and Weyerhaeuser timber,[104] welcoming another extension by President Bush of China's MFN, addressing a variety of local and national audiences on China, traveling to China and Hong Kong with William A. Glassford, the Council president and senior vice president of Security Pacific Bank Washington, and putting on another China Trade Update conference. Abnett also began to think if the Council could expand its spheres of attention to include Hong Kong, Singapore and Taiwan to reduce its dependence of trade activity with China by becoming the "Chinese Relations Council."[105]

---

101. Washington State China Relations Council archives.
102. Jim Mann, "A touch choice: American jobs or Chinese rights?" *The Seattle Times*, Jul. 23, 1991
103. The Seattle Times, "Breaking The Ice," Feb. 25, 1991
104. Tom Brown, "China 'Spends' The Day," *The Seattle Times*, Jun. 1, 1991
105. Steve Wilhelm, "Expanded scope urged for China council," *Puget Sound Business Journal*, Jan. 24, 1992

Toward the end of the year, however, Abnett decided to resign. One could try to understand why from the 1991 annual report by Mr. Glassford even without any personal reasons on Abnett's part:

> "…The deteriorating bilateral relationship between U.S. and China; the now annual Congressional debates over MFN status for China; the economic slow-down in China; lingering public sentiments of the 1989 Tiananmen Square tragedy; and the U.S. recession…The Council's membership revenues declined again…

> "…But at this time, it was strongly felt that the basic elements of the Council's existence had not changed; our state is a leader in trade with China; despite the current economic and political difficulties, China is of paramount importance to our state's interests in the long run…"[106]

In the short run, however, the Council had to eliminate the position of program associate and contract its management to WCIT, with which the Council had shared office space, reference materials, and office machines since October 1987. The Council also decided to have Robert Kapp, the WCIT president, serving as its part-time executive director for at least the remainder of 1992.

After leaving the Council, Abnett opened his own consulting business and also did some teaching. Over the past decade or so, Abnett has been the senior advisor on China projects at the National Bureau of Asian Research, a Seattle-based non-profit, nonpartisan research institution. He has also been running an online forum: China-WTO Forum, hosting discussions of key U.S. policymakers and select specialists in academic and business communities on topics of China and the WTO, his field of expertise.

I have made attempts to interview Abnett for this chapter. But the attempts did not succeed. It may be better this way, for reminiscing could be painful. Abnett did, however, make available to me the two photos used in the chapter.

---

106. Washington State China Relations Council archives.

William B. Abnett, 2004

2.3

Eden Woon—From Math to Mass Commerce
(Executive Director, 1994–1997)

Eden Y. Woon, 1994

It may not be hard to find someone who is an American success story or a Chinese success story. But it may not be easy to find someone who is both an American success story and a Chinese success story. I found one, however, in Eden Woon, the third executive director of the Washington State China Relations Council. As Woon himself said once, he had a foot in two worlds—the Untied States and China.

At the time of this writing, Mr. Woon is still in Hong Kong, having just started his ninth year as the CEO of the Hong Kong General Chamber of Commerce, the position he first took over back in late-May 1997, straight from the Council.

I have never met Mr. Woon. But I did follow major changes and developments at the Council over the years. I remember reading a special opinion by Woon, as the Council executive director, in the Seattle Times in the mid-1990s. That was a first, because I don't remember any other directors writing opinions in newspapers. Woon is also easy to remember for he was the only Chinese-American director the Council ever had.

I was eager to find out about his Chinese-American story. With an introduction by Mr. Joseph Borich beforehand, I sent Woon an email to his address at the Chamber in Hong Kong. I asked a number of background questions such as family, childhood, schools, languages, etc. But Woon, with the typical modesty of a person of Chinese cultural heritage, said that he would help me with the project but preferred addressing questions dealing with his work at the Council, not his background and personality.

Well, I understood but still preferred finding some "personality" information about Woon. Luckily for me, with the help of Google, I found some at the website of his alma mater—the College of Arts & Sciences of the University of Washington. I am sure Woon would forgive me, and Google.

Born in Shanghai, China, little Eden was two when his family moved to Hong Kong. A decade later, the family immigrated to the United States. In 1972, Woon, as his parents must have expected their son to, received his Ph.D in mathematics from the University of Washington. It was the same university with which two other former directors of the Council, Robert Kapp and William Abnett, were also associated around the time, the former in teaching and latter in graduate school.

With his doctoral degree, Woon went on to a steady academic career, teaching mathematics at the U.S. Air Force Academy through the 1970s and early 1980s. As an associate professor of mathematics, Woon didn't seem to have China much on his mind, at least professionally.

But Woon was about to make a change, the first of several major career changes from then on, each one bringing him closer, higher and deeper into the China field.

The year was 1983 when Woon got an offer, very different from teaching at the academy, to work in the American embassy in Beijing. And Woon took it. How did he make that transition from teaching to diplomacy? As Woon recalled to his alma mater: "It was when China first opened up and its relationship with the U.S. was just beginning…Technology transfer to China was a big concern. I had the technical background to deal with technology issues and I was a native speaker, so I was appointed first assistant air attaché in the American embassy."[107]

And there, at the embassy, Woon was also to become a friend as well as colleague to his predecessor William Abnett, who was serving as chief of the Economic Affairs Section there from 1982–1985.

In the summer of 1983, soon after his arrival in Beijing, Woon went to work preparing for Secretary of Defense Casper Weinberger's visit to China. It was a historic visit. During the visit, Secretary Weinberger announced the new "three pillars" program of security cooperation between the United States and China, including comprehensive high level visits, functional exchanges and the sale of U.S. defensive weapons, military equipment, and technology to China.[108] As a result, Woon played a role in developing those cooperative programs involving the U.S. and Chinese military. "It was a very interesting time to be there," Woon said about the work, "It was extremely useful to be a native speaker, able to talk with people very naturally in Chinese."[109]

In the spring of the following year, 1984, President Reagan visited China, too.

---

107. College of Arts & Sciences, University of Washington, "A China Expert Returns to His Childhood Home," http://www.artsci.washington.edu/newsletter/Winter99/China.html

108. Thomas L. Wilborn, "Security Cooperation with China: Analysis And A Proposal," http://www.carlisle.army.mil/ssi/pdffiles/PUB99.pdf

109. College of Arts & Sciences, University of Washington, "A China Expert Returns to His Childhood Home," http://www.artsci.washington.edu/newsletter/Winter99/China.html

One could imagine how those two visits and two years working at the embassy at a time of growing U.S.-China rapprochement changed our math-professor-turned-military-attaché. Within a few months of returning to a scientific analyst job at the Pentagon, Woon decided to quit mathematics once and for all. He felt that he could be more useful and contribute more in the area of China policy work.

Woon soon became the China policy adviser in the office of the Joint Chiefs of Staff, advising on military relations with China. A few years later, in 1989, Woon rose to become the China adviser in the office of the secretary of defense, the top China job in the Department of Defense. For the next five years, Woon was responsible for formulating policy positions and recommendations on all issues related to China that affected the Department of Defense.

In 1993, Air Force Colonel Woon decided to retire from the military, but not from the Pentagon. He stayed on at the Pentagon as a civilian for another year and accompanied Secretary of Defense William Perry to China in 1994. It was another historic visit, the first by an American secretary of defense to China after the Tiananmen event in 1989.

It was, however, time to change again, as Woon told his alma mater, "I wanted to leave the defense and security relationship with China but continue my involvement with China in some other way. I also wanted to come back to Seattle, which I really missed."[110]

In fact, Woon had often returned to Seattle to visit friends and to hike in the Cascades. He had also been invited back to Seattle to speak to the Washington State China Relations Council. In November 1990, while Abnett was the executive director, Woon was one of the guest speakers at the Council's annual China Trade Update conference, briefing on political, economic, business and legal conditions in China. That was a year and a half after Tiananmen.

At that conference, Woon talked about steps the Bush administration had taken to oppose the killings in China, steps ranging from cuts in military exchanges to the outright ban of sales of ammunition and high technology. He also pointed out the positive steps taken by China, from lifting martial law to

---

110. Ibid.

releasing detainees, from allowing U.S. diplomats access to Tibet to restoring participation in the Fulbright scholar program and inviting the Peace Corps into the country. On business with China, Woon said that in the short run, the prospect for increased trade opportunities was not too positive. But in the long run, in the 1990s, doing business with China might get easier for U.S. businesses. In the end, Woon added, "The world of the '90s is different than that of the 1950s. It's an interlocking community."[111]

What exactly Woon meant by the world being an interlocking community would become clearer later on. In November 1994, however, that understanding plus his eleven years in the China field, from diplomacy to policy advising, won him kudos from the board of the Council. In announcing that Woon was succeeding the part-time Kapp on December 1st as the next executive director, Michael Bickford, Council president and director of corporate positioning of Weyerhaeuser Company, said that, being fluent in Mandarin and Cantonese, Woon would "help guide the council's efforts in enhancing our understanding and relationship in China."[112]

Coinciding with Woon's arrival in Seattle early that November, and perhaps as a welcome to Woon to the Washington state-China scene, the Washington State China Relations Council and the US-China Business Council, with Kapp as the new president, were jointly hosting a dinner in Seattle in mid November for a high-profile Chinese delegation headed by Mr. Li Lanqing, vice premier responsible for China's foreign trade. With the delegation's new order of 2,100 American minivans, a $1.6 billion deal with McDonnell Douglas and talk of more orders for Boeing airplanes,[113] the atmosphere in Seattle that night was very good, and had come a long way from that chilly winter greeting four years earlier for the controversial Chinese trade conference.

Woon must have felt good starting the new job at the time, not just because of the atmosphere around Vice Premier Li's visit, but more importantly because of the encouraging trade figures. In 1994, Washington state's exports to China totaled $2.2 billion while the imports from China reached $5.8 billion, making

---

111. Polly Lane, "China, US Take The Long View," *The Seattle Times*, Nov. 6, 1990
112. Staff, "Eden Woon Is New Director Of China Relations Council," *The Seattle Times*, Nov. 5, 1994
113. Evelyn Iritani, "Red Carpet For China Dignitary Boeing, Governor Woo Senior Official For Trade," *Seattle Post-Intelligencer*, Nov. 12, 1994, p. B1

the two-way trade a whopping $8 billion,[114]more than three times that of 1989, the year of Tiananmen!

But Woon had to start his directorship from a low point, including a low point in the Council membership. The Tiananmen event and the adjustment that the Council had to make in its aftermath had plunged the Council membership to 57, nearly back to the initial number of membership in 1980. By hiring him on a full-time basis, Woon told me in an email, the board was committing to regenerate the Council and make it prominent again in China trade. Woon was going to make that happen. He was going to get the membership back up, too.

Judging from the quantity of the Council newsletters he wrote from early 1995 to early 1997, Woon was a diligent and hard-working director. First, breaking the tradition of Kapp and Abnett in writing quarterly newsletters, Woon started his as "Monthly Updates." Second, he filled those updates with information, from membership to programs, from policy issues to announcements. The most important content was, of course, the programs, with which Woon packed each month's calendar, for members as well as the community.

In the February 1995 "Monthly Updates," for instance, Woon announced four programs from Feb. 22 to Mar. 20. There was a briefing by Woon on his trip to Washington D.C. to discuss China problems with administration officials; there was the annual banquet featuring the general counsel of Secretary of Commerce Ron Brown; there was a co-sponsored reception with WCIT for visitors from China and other regions; and there was a seminar and a luncheon with Lu Ping, the top China official in charge of Hong Kong affairs, and his delegation. That was one program a week!

In that newsletter, Woon urged Council members to mark the calendar for the seminar and luncheon with Lu Ping for it was a rare opportunity for them to ask questions about China's Hong Kong policy after 1997. Hong Kong had been scheduled to return to China on July 1, 1997, after being under British rule for 150 years. Hong Kong was also a special place for Woon, the place of his childhood.

---

114. Stanley Holmes, Stephen H. Dunphy, "State Does Big Business With China," *The Seattle Times*, Mar. 12, 1996.

"The socialism of the mainland will not be practiced in Hong Kong," Mr. Lu told the members of the Council at the luncheon in Seattle's Madison Hotel, "The previous capitalist system and way of life shall remain unchanged for 50 years. We'll have one country and two systems."[115] Lu also assured the audience that Hong Kong would remain a free port; a separate customs territory with its own convertible currency; a global financial center with markets for foreign exchange, gold, securities and futures; a jurisdiction with laws protecting private property and foreign investments; and an independent participant in international organizations such as the World Trade Organization.

That was an encouraging message. In addition to its important role in U.S.-China trade in general as a center of processing, transshipping and other services as Woon's predecessor Abnett had testified before Congress, Hong Kong was also a growing trade partner of Washington state. In 1994, Washington trade with Hong Kong was about $1.1 billion each in exports and imports and as much as three-fourths of the apples from Washington to China were transshipped through Hong Kong.[116] Because of those roles, Hong Kong had also become dependent on China's MFN trade status with the United States for its economic prosperity. In the words of a representative of Jardine Matheson, the British trading house that had helped found modern Hong Kong, their luck went up and down with MFN.[117]

Therefore, in the next two years' run-up to Hong Kong's transition from Britain to China, Woon had a number of Council programs devoted to the subject.

In October 1995, Roderick Woo, president of the Hong Kong Law Society, talked to Council members about common law in Hong Kong after 1997. In May 1996, Woon and representatives from Boeing, Microsoft, Seafirst Bank, the Port of Seattle and others were part of a Seattle delegation headed by the Greater Seattle Chamber of Commerce on a study mission to Hong Kong. Late that month, the Council hosted in Seattle Anson Chan, chief secretary of the Hong Kong government and principal adviser to then Governor Chris Patten, on her speaking tour in the U.S. In January 1997, John Kamm, former president of the

---

115. Imbert Matthee, "China Gives Assurance On Hong Kong Business Interests Secure, Envoy Says," *Seattle Post-Intelligencer*, Mar. 21, 1995, p. B5

116. Stephen H. Dunphy, "Operation Hong Kong," *The Seattle Times*, May 5, 1996

117. Imbert Matthee, "Hong Kong Most Fears A Trade War Between China, U.S." *Seattle Post-Intelligencer*, May 10, 1996, p. A1

American Chamber of Commerce in Hong Kong, spoke at a Council luncheon on how the business community could help improve the Chinese human rights situation. In March 1997, Richard Boucher, then U.S. consul general in Hong Kong, gave a luncheon talk on "How the U.S. Sees the Hong Kong Transition." There was also, that month, Ronnie Chan, a well-known Hong Kong business-man, speaking at the Council's annual banquet on "Hong Kong After 1997: A Hong Kong Businessman's Perspective."[118]

In the May 1996 newsletter, Woon wrote his impression on the Hong Kong issue:

> "In Hong Kong, the 90-member Seattle delegation…met with influential business and civic leaders, who almost unanimously expressed confidence in the turnover to Chinese sovereignty and bullish on post-1997 Hong Kong…
>
> "The speakers also were worried about US congressional interest in Hong Kong…In sum, you could say that we found that Hong Kong was more wor-ried about the US and MFN than about China and 1997."[119]

Yes, Hong Kong was worried about China's MFN. But so were the businesses in Washington state, especially the Council members. Woon fully understood that. He was ready to continue the Council's mission of lobbying for the exten-sion of China's MFN, and devote a lot of time to it, too. The following, as recorded in the newsletters, shows exactly how much and how hard Woon had lobbied.

1995—

February: Not even two months at the Council, Woon took a trip to Wash-ington, D.C. to discuss China problems with administration officials and the Washington State congressional delegation.

May: Woon sent a Council letter to President Clinton urging continuation of de-linking China's MFN and human rights.

---

118. Washington State China Relations Council archives.
119. Ibid.

Early July: Woon talked to Washington's congressional delegation, wrote to legislators urging them to renew China's MFN status, and urged Council members to write individual company letters to their representatives.

July 21: The day after the House had passed a bill not overruling the President's decision to renew MFN for China, Woon wrote his congratulations in a special newsletter:

> "We are all obviously relieved, and I have been told by our congressional delegation that the Council's lobbying effort and efforts of individual companies in this state had an impact on our legislators. Thank you for your support."[120]

1996–

February: Woon had Lee Sands, Assistant U.S. Trade Representative and the point man for all trade negotiations with China, speaking to a Council luncheon on China's intellectual property rights issue and his take on MFN renewal and WTO entry by China.

Later that month, Woon was in Washington, D.C. As he wrote in that month's newsletter,

> "...not only does the Council provide information in a variety of ways to help the members do business with China, but we spend a lot of effort with Congress and the administration being a voice on behalf of the members for maintaining sound trade relations with China."[121]

March: Woon gave his take in the Council newsletter on the possible vote in the House and Senate to deny China's MFN and urged members to be vigilant and contact legislators. He warned, "...MFN is the biggest problem. The situation is tense, and the stakes are large. We need to help each other to get through this."[122]

---

120. Washington State China Relations Council archives.
121. Ibid.
122. Ibid.

April: Woon spoke to Congressman Rick White about MFN and encouraged members of Congress to visit companies in their home district to get a personal sense of the impact of MFN revocation.

Mid-April: Woon had Mike Lampton of the National Committee on US-China Relations speaking to the Council on that year's MFN fight.

Later that month, Woon wrote a special opinion on the importance of China's MFN in the Seattle Times, presenting testimonials of four small local businesses that depended on China for 25 to 100 percent of their growth. He wrote:

> "As I travel around this state, I have found numerous businesses either engaged with or interested in China, the fastest-growing economy of the world. Whether they are in agriculture, manufacturing, services, import, retail, high-tech, transportation, or whether they are large-, medium-, or small-sized, they have all made strategic calculations to work the China market for the next 20 years..."[123]

Woon ended by suggesting permanent MFN for China, probably the first such suggestion by a Council director:

> "Businesses succeed in China when they first develop a good relationship with their Chinese counterpart before discussing the details of a transaction. Why can't our government take a page from our businesses' playbook and first develop a China policy that establishes a constructive framework that includes permanent MFN extension?"[124]

May: Woon talked to Sen. Slade Gorton and his staff several times about MFN.

June: Woon had Chinese Ambassador Li Daoyu speaking to a Council dinner at the Westin Hotel on the necessity to establish permanent MFN status to end the yearly debates, and the benefit of cooperation between United States and China to economic development and in regional and world peace.

---

123. Eden Y. Woon, "China's Too Vital To Be Treated This Way," *The Seattle Times*, Apr. 24, 1996
124. Ibid.

Woon then talked to Rep. Linda Smith, Rep. Doc Hastings, Sen. Patty Murray, and Rep. Jennifer Dunn about MFN.

Woon also informed members that an agreement had been reached at the eleventh hour on the intellectual property rights violation issue with China, avoiding sanctions against China that could have brought a crisis in U.S.-China trade.

July: Woon was in D.C. again and saw MFN extended. In that month's newsletter, Woon wrote with excitement:

> "China MFN is safe for one more year. All of you should congratulate yourselves for your letters and the work you have done in preserving our important trade relationship with China."[125]

In the same newsletter, Woon also told the members of a new development on the issue of China's permanent MFN. When Assistant Secretary of State Winston Lord testified in the Senate, Woon wrote, he was asked by several senators, Why don't we renew MFN for China for good? Woon gladly informed the members that he had met both Sen. Patty Murray and Rep. Jennifer Dunn who had agreed to pursue the issue of permanent MFN for China in Congress.

August: Woon further discussed the issue of MFN with the members. He wrote in the newsletter, "…there is a growing awareness of the inappropriateness of the MFN tool on China policy and the 'most favored nation' misnomer…What we really would like to see, however, is *permanent* MFN for China, not just a change-of-name…Congress should get rid of the annual MFN debate."[126]

September: Woon was in D.C. to attend a strategy conference on obtaining permanent MFN for China. He happily reported after return that several congressmen and senators had voiced support for such a move. Better still, he informed the members that the Senate had already passed a bill changing 'MFN' to 'NTS'—'normal trading status,' and the House would soon follow suit.[127]

---

125. Washington State China Relations Council archives.
126. Ibid.
127. Ibid.

December: Woon was in D.C. again, meeting with Lee Sands, USTR's principal WTO negotiator with China, and with the Commerce Department China director.

1997–

March: Woon accompanied Sen. Murray and 16 Washington state business people to China. A strong supporter of China MFN, Sen. Murray met with Vice Premier Li Lanqing, who had visited Seattle two years earlier, and came away from Beijing more convinced than ever that trade ties with China must be maintained.

April: One month before taking over as the next director of the Hong Kong General Chamber of Commerce, Woon traveled to Washington, D.C. once more. However, he said, "I found my visit to DC quite depressing..." Woon wrote in the monthly newsletter,

> "...with the administration hunkering down with the barrage of allegations on Chinese campaign financing, and Congress in an anti-China mood fueled by an alliance of human rights activists, religious activists, security buffs who talk of a China threat, anti-communist ideologues, labor unions fearful of losing jobs, people who view the Hong Kong transition with concern, Tibetan independence supporters, and those in the Republican party who want to make China Clinton's albatross."[128]

Woon urged members to write Sen. Gorton with their support of MFN for China.

May: "MFN for China is under attack again in Congress," Woon warned members, and urged them once more to write to their congressmen on the importance of renewing MFN for China with anecdotes and specific examples of jobs and benefits tied to China trade. "Perhaps in the end," Woon wrote in the newsletter,

> "Congress will realize that despite all the political rhetoric, removing MFN from China is not in the U.S. interest. Congress has learned this same lesson

---

128. Ibid.

for seven years now, but let us not simply assume that it will do the right thing this time…"[129]

Woon pushed for China's MFN throughout his tenure at the Council until the last minute of his stay in Seattle.

There had been other issues in those years, however, that had complicated China's MFN, as well as Woon's work, such as that of Taiwan.

In February 1995, as Woon recorded in the "Policy" section of the "Monthly Updates," Olympia was considering a petition to Washington, D.C., on the admission of Taiwan to U.N and a resolution to enter into a sister-state relationship with Taiwan, the "Republic of China." Woon was clearly opposed to such moves. He told the members that the Council had been lobbying against the petition and the term "ROC" in the sister-state resolution. He explained further,

> "We feel there is no need for the state to get embroiled in the knotty foreign policy issue between China, the U.S. and Taiwan. So far, the Taiwan lobby has been very strong. It does not hurt for our members to express their views to their respective state legislators."[130]

To Woon's delight, both bills on Taiwan died that year. But the Taiwan issue would come up again, and again.

In May 1995, the State Department issued a visa to Lee Teng-hui, then president of Taiwan, to visit the United States. China protested it as an infringement upon China's sovereignty, a violation of the principles of the three Sino-U.S. joint communiqués and a serious damage to Sino-U.S. relations.[131] In March 1996, before Taiwan's presidential election, China conducted war games and test-fired missiles into the Taiwan Strait to express its dissatisfaction over the Taiwan leader's tendency towards independence. The U.S. advised caution and restraint and sent two aircraft carrier task forces to within about 200 miles of the east coast of Taiwan.

---

129. Ibid.
130. Ibid.
131. Washington Post, "China Halts N-Talks Over Taiwanian Visit," *The Seattle Times*, May 29, 1995

As Woon wrote in the newsletter that month, "Just when you think US-China relations cannot possibly be worse, another crisis comes to the forefront to send things downward one more notch."[132]

That month, on the very subject, Taiwan, Woon organized the Council's annual banquet and invited the former Assistant Secretary of Defense for international security affairs, Charles Freeman, to be the keynote speaker. A longtime China expert, Mr. Freeman told the members that the United States should continue its referee role between China and Taiwan, not playing the game itself. Praising the "strategic ambiguity" towards Taiwan, Freeman said the Clinton administration needed to rebuild its communications with Beijing and Taipei to head off further escalation of the crisis.[133]

Woon gave members his own observation of the situation in the newsletter,

"...not only is there additional negative feeling about China generated from the tension in the Taiwan Strait, there is the possibility of real military conflict erupting. That, of course, would be disastrous for our trade with either China or Taiwan. I remain hopeful that the threats by China are just that, threats, and that after the March 23 election in Taiwan, both sides will renew cross-Strait dialogue, and stability will once again prevail in that region, and everybody gets back to the business of business."[134]

Fortunately, no military conflict erupted in Taiwan Strait and everybody went back to the business of business. Still there were issues other than Taiwan that Woon had to tackle with—for example, human rights.

In July 1995, Harry Wu, former Chinese labor camp inmate, naturalized U.S. citizen and human rights activist, was detained in China on charges of spying, stealing state secrets and trying to enter the country under an assumed name. The U.S. government protested. In the "Monthly Updates," Woon wrote:

"US-China relations are at a very low ebb. After the visit of Taiwan's Lee Teng-hui, the already tense relationship was exacerbated by the arrest of Harry Wu...This has given new fuel to those in Congress who want to withdraw

132. Washington State China Relations Council archives.
133. Imbert Matthee, "U.S. Shares Blame For Tensions, Ex-Advisor Says," *Seattle Post-Intelligencer*, Mar. 6, 1996, p. A12
134. Washington State China Relations Council archives.

China's MFN status. A vote on the House floor is taking place around July 19, and it is going to be close. I have been talking to our congressional delegation...but I don't have to tell you how disastrous it would be for trade with China if MFN is revoked."[135]

With diplomatic maneuvering, however, Harry Wu was later expelled. In December that year, Harry Wu came to Seattle and spoke in Auburn to 300 striking members of the International Association of Machinists and Aerospace Workers against Boeing. Wu blasted Boeing for doing business with China and being silent on human rights abuses,[136] and said the United States needed a China policy somewhere between the U.S. policy of "containment" of the former Soviet Union and President Clinton's "engagement', and link trade and political reform in China instead of giving the country "a free lunch."[137]

Woon disagreed with the dissident's approach. He spoke out, to a local paper, defending Boeing, the oldest and largest member of the Council, as well as China trade.

"No one is trying to minimize the number of problems that need to be addressed. However, what we don't need is an emotional lumping together of problems that aren't related."[138]

Woon emphasized that it's better to include China in the world economy rather than isolate it and pointed out how China's economic interaction with the West had already led to positive change, he said, "You cannot argue with the fact that the general livelihood of the average Chinese citizen and some basic freedoms have improved dramatically during the past 10 years."[139]

In January 1997, a group of members of the Seattle-based consumer cooperative Recreational Equipment, Inc. (REI), with the help of the Tibetan Rights Campaign of Seattle, was calling for a boycott of REI goods labeled "Made in

---

135. Ibid.
136. Stanley Holmes, "Dissident Blasts Boeing's Trade Of Jobs For Jets," *The Seattle Times*, Dec. 2, 1995
137. Imbert Matthee, "Wu Says Boeing Is Bowing To Chinese," *Seattle Post-Intelligencer*, Dec. 1, 1995
138. Ibid.
139. Ibid.

China." The company had imported $10 million worth of goods from China in 1996 for its nationwide chain of 46 stores and 1.4 million members.[140]

Woon, not believing in linking trade and human rights as Harry Wu did, came out again and spoke. Northwest retailers, he said to a local paper, who always made sure they did business with Chinese factories that met ethical and labor standards, used to worry only about the annual renewal of most-favored-nation trading status for China. "But now, there is a new pressure formed by a coalition of labor and human rights activists. This pressure, which brings in other political problems with China, is ill-advised."[141]

That was how Woon stayed firm and clear about the Council's mission in those controversial times. But were there high times, good times, for Woon? Yes, of course.

I asked Woon his most memorable event at the Council. Just as I had guessed, Woon said it was the appearance at the Council in late 1995 of his former boss at the Pentagon, Secretary of Defense William Perry, as the distinguished luncheon speaker. He told me in an email,

> "The membership thrilled to his speech on U.S.-China relations, the attention Secretary Perry paid to the Council and the buzz and energy among the crowd were very rewarding to me."

It was on October 30, and more than 320 business and political leaders of Washington state packed the Four Seasons in Seattle to hear Secretary Perry. With "seriousness, thoughtfulness, and intelligence," as Woon described in the monthly newsletter, Secretary Perry said, in his speech, that the United States and China must continue to seek common political and military interests in Asia despite disagreements over Chinese human rights abuses and Taiwan's future, and,

> "Engagement does not mean that we will ignore those issues. Engagement recognizes that the best way to change those policies we don't like is through firm

---

140. Imbert Matthee, "REI Faces China Question," *Seattle Post-Intelligencer*, Jan. 10, 1997, p. B1
141. Ibid.

diplomacy and dialogue. Even when we strongly disagree with China, we cannot make our entire policy hostage to a single issue."[142]

Woon felt very encouraged by that speech. It showed in the newsletter:

"As you know, 'China as a threat' has been a favorite theme of journalists and academicians in recent months, and 'containment' has been advocated as a China policy by some. Secretary Perry dismissed this type of negative thinking and argued forcefully for 'engagement." Those who do business with China can only applaud this constructive engagement."[143]

Woon did not just applaud engagement. He believed in it and had carried it out in Council activities throughout his tenure.

It was with all those activities and his hard work, including programs, meetings, trips, media exposure, speeches, and newsletters, that Woon was able to add new members to the Council each and every month. By the end of 1995, the membership rose to 123, from 57. By October 1996, it reached 158. A couple months later, in January 1997, it reached the Council record: 180.[144] Woon did it! He brought the Council membership up from an all-time low to an all-time high in two years.

Not only did Woon bring the membership back up, he also made the regeneration of the Council a reality. As he wrote in his farewell notes in the last of his Council newsletter in May 1997:

"A new Executive Director will be in place this summer sometime. He or she will take over an organization in a healthy financial situation, sound membership base, widely known in China, Hong Kong, and respected in Washington D.C. and Olympia."

Woon must have felt good with his record. Who wouldn't? He continued:

"I leave the Washington State China Relations Council with fond memories of the members, the programs, the trips, the business meetings, and the

142. Ed Offley, "Perry Defends Policy On China 'Engagement Is Best Strategy,'" *Seattle Post-Intelligencer*, Oct. 31, 1995, p. A2
143. Washington State China Relations Council archives.
144. Ibid.

friendship of everyone with whom I worked in my two and one half years with the Council. Thanks to a terrific staff and an outstanding Executive Committee, I think we have been able to serve the members in ways they expect."[145]

Woon is still thankful today to the people with whom he worked. In his response to one of my emails, Woon told me not to forget the staff and interns who were there from 1994 to 1997 when he was the executive director.

Woon did work with more staff and interns than his predecessors, as I found out. Among them, at different times, were Catherine Lanham, program services manager; Alexis Albion, program and research assistant; Eric Samuels, volunteer intern; Caroline Wei, volunteer intern; Stephanie Baldwin, volunteer intern; Alaina Sparks, intern; Kelsey Fuller, intern; Jamie Clausen, summer intern; and Hillary Haselton, office administrator. It was with the help of Jamie Clausen that the Council got its first home page in October 1996, with the address at http://www.eskimo.com/~wscrc. The Council also got its first email address back in April that year at WSCRC@aol.com.

Woon also has nothing but praises for Mic Dinsmore, the president of the Council in both 1995 and 1996 and executive director (Now CEO) of the Port of Seattle. Dinsmore was a terrific leader, Woon told me in an email, who knew where he wanted to lead the Council, gave Woon full support to carry out that strategy, and helped a lot in raising the Council's profile and bringing in members. No doubt, Dinsmore and Woon were a terrific team.

What was his most satisfying experience at the Council? I asked gingerly, for it might be a little personal. But the question was OK. Woon said it was to be able to help members connect in China business or provide them information that would be useful to their business.

I got bolder and asked him another "personal" question. Did he feel that with his Chinese-American background, he understood U.S.-China relations better than others? Woon gave me a longer answer:

"Don't want to compare myself with others…But my work in the U.S. government on China, including participation in MFN debates even in Washington, helped me understand China policy by the U.S. and how the government

---

145. Ibid.

and ordinary people think about China. My ease of dealing with the Chinese from my years of work with them before, made it easy to build relations with the commercial and policy sectors in China. I thoroughly enjoyed my job."

Wow, thoroughly! Woon commented again on the excellent support given him from the top in the board and from the bottom among the smallest members. Finally, he revealed something more "personal" than I had expected. He wrote:

> "I always wanted to achieve this goal: That people would say, 'I heard Washington State China Relations Council had a great event last night. I am sorry I wasn't there.' I think we came close to achieving that."

I am sure Mr. Dinsmore and the Council's executive committees agreed with him on that.

In 1997, William Glassford, senior vice president of Seafirst Bank, took over as the president of the Council. While Mr. Glassford was looking for a replacement for Woon, Woon was already the new CEO of the Hong Kong General Chamber of Commerce. He got in right before the historic handover of Hong Kong from Britain to China on July 1, 1997. He left behind many contacts he had helped build for Washington state businesses in Hong Kong as well as in other parts of China.

If one didn't fully understand what Woon meant by the "interlocking community" of the world back in 1990, the fact that Woon became the first non-British, ethnic Chinese and American CEO of the 144-year-old and 4,000-member-strong Hong Kong General Chamber of Commerce, and has held that position for more than eight years, further explains it.

That "interlocking" is fully illustrated by Woon's path: from Shanghai to Hong Kong to Seattle, from Washington D.C. to Seattle and to Hong Kong again, from China to U.S. and U.S. to China, and from math to military to mass commerce.

Eden Y. Woon, 2005

2.4

Joseph Borich—Into the 21st Century
(Executive Director, 1997–)

Joseph J. Borich, 1997

After tracing the steps of the founders to 1979 and then following those of the three directors through the 1980s and most of the 1990s, I have come back to where I started—Joseph J. Borich, the current executive director of the Washington State China Relations Council.

I met Mr. Borich for the first time a few years ago in Seattle's Chinatown. We shared a table at a dinner in honor of an environmental group from China. He was friendly, easy-going, no airs at all. I told him that I was from Shaanxi. He said his wife's mother was also from Shaanxi. Last April, when Lien Chan, Chairman of the Nationalist Party in Taiwan, visited his primary school in Xi'an while on a historic trip to China, I told Borich in an email that Lien Chan's primary school was also mine. Borich said his wife's mother had gone to school there, too. It was a small world, he added. It did seem so.

Starting in August 1997, replacing Eden Woon, Borich has served as the executive director at the Council continuously since. I have a feeling that Borich will soon be replacing Mr. Robert Kapp as Council's longest-serving executive director, with no breaks. Borich also holds a unique title all by himself, the turn-of-the-century-director.

On May 29, 1997, announcing Borich's hiring, William A. Glassford, Council president from 1997 to 1999 and senior vice president of Seafirst Bank, said, "He is a terrific find."[146] Patricia Davis, president of WCIT, commented this way, "He's really impressive. He knows China up and down. And he's very good with people."[147] There was an interesting headline in a local paper the following day, "China Council Recruits China Consul."[148] I thought that was fun.

But Borich's career was far more fun than that headline. By the time he moved to Seattle, Borich had already had a 24-year career with the U.S. Foreign Service. He had in fact served under every president from Nixon to Clinton in a China-related capacity. Again in Mr. Glassford's words, "Borich brought strong governmental and Chinese business experience to benefit both the China Relations Council and Washington State."[149]

That "Chinese" experience, however, meant "Chinese" on both sides of the Taiwan Strait. As a local paper described, Borich was as a senior foreign-policy executive with strong China and Taiwan expertise, having spent a good part of his diplomatic career crisscrossing the Taiwan Strait.[150] He served first in the U.S. mission in Taipei from 1973 to 1975, then at the China desk at the State Department from 1975 to 1978. He went on to head the commercial section at the U.S. consulate in Shanghai from 1980 to 1982, having helped open the con-

146. Imbert Matthee, "U.S. Envoy In China Will Head Group Here," Seattle Post-Intelligencer, May 30, 1997
147. Ibid.
148. Puget Sound Business Journal, "Latest News," May 30, 1997
149. Ibid.
150. Ron Redmond, "Village Elections Can Lead To Major Changes In China," *Seattle Post-Intelligencer*, Dec. 14, 1998, p. A2

sulate first. From 1982 to 1986 he worked again in Taipei, and from 1994 to 1997, he was the American consul general in Shanghai.[151]

But Borich's career was not all fun. He served in harm's way, too. From 1969 to 1971, Borich was a member in the U.S. Army and served a tour in Vietnam. Sergeant Borich was a military advisor to Vietnamese regional forces. With that, Borich is the fourth veteran among the Council founders and directors after Richard Kirk, William Abnett and Eden Woon. But that was not all. From 1990 to 1993, Borich was the deputy chief of mission at the U.S. embassy in Mogadishu, Somalia, of all places. He was among the last 20 people to evacuate, after closing the embassy there, with the U.S. Navy providing military cover and helicopters. The rest of America of course learned about the fierce and tragic Battle of Mogadishu of October 1993 on television, and later in the movie "Black Hawk Down."

We are all glad that Borich emerged safely from Mogadishu. But how did Borich get to know the Council? It turned out that Borich had spoken at a Council luncheon before. He and Eden Woon had also known each other since early 1980s when Woon was in Beijing and Borich was in Shanghai. In fact, the two had frequently worked together in the early 1990s in an interagency group analyzing Taiwan policy, particularly that of arms sales to Taiwan. At that time, Borich was the director of Taiwan coordination staff in the Bureau of East Asian and Pacific Affairs at the State Department and Woon was still at the Pentagon. Woon, as the executive director, had also taken two Council groups to Shanghai during 1995–96.

The aforementioned luncheon was on May 23, 1996, when Borich, as then consul general in Shanghai, was in Seattle at the invitation of Woon. The topic Borich briefed the Council audience on? Pudong New District of Shanghai, of course, the overnight economic and financial sensation on the east bank of the Huangpu River. He also gave an account of the overall business climate of Shanghai and welcomed all Council members to contact his office for information or assistance.[152]

Whether or not Council members contacted him in Shanghai, Borich must have left the Council with a very good impression. It was coincidental that a year later when Woon was leaving for Hong Kong, Borich's service in Shanghai was

151. Imbert Matthee, "U.S. Envoy In China Will Head Group Here," *Seattle Post-Intelligencer*, May 30, 1997
152. Washington State China Relations Council newsletter, June 1996

coming to an end, too. It was all so fitting that the Council offered Borich the position of the executive director and Borich accepted. With Shanghai, China's largest city, fast becoming the business center of China and overtaking Hong Kong, and with Washington State having just opened a trade office in Shanghai the year before, who could be a better choice than Borich to bring the Council the needed new perspective?

The fact that Borich and his Taiwan-born wife Hsiao-hui liked Seattle also helped. But no sooner had the Boriches settled into their new home than Borich was asked by Governor Gary Locke to be his China advisor on his early October trade mission to China. It was Gov. Locke's first trip to China after being elected in November 1996, and he was traveling with a large delegation, including the official party, staff, family, and several dozen business and community representatives. For Borich, the trip was a good start and a consolidation of his new job at the Council.

The delegation went to Beijing, Chengdu and Shanghai. In Beijing, Gov. Locke had a meeting with Chinese President Jiang Zemin, an honor not given to every visiting governor. In Chengdu, he met the governor of Sichuan and in Shanghai, the mayor. To Borich, Shanghai felt like home and one he was proud to show off. As he was quoted, "For China, the 21st century is in Shanghai."[153]

As we all know, Gov. Locke ended that trade mission on a highly emotional note by visiting Jilong, his ancestral village in Taishan County, Guangdong Province.

One day after returning from China with the governor, Borich was off to Skamania Lodge in Stevenson, WA to preside over the conference on "U.S. China Relations in the 21st Century." Co-sponsored by the Council and the American Assembly, it was attended by over 40 executives, scholars, and politicians from the West Coast.

In his first Council newsletter of October 1997, Borich mentioned the conference and then went on to report on the governor's trip,

> "...the Governor's visit struck me as highly successful. In China, he was accorded the treatment normally reserved for visiting presidents and premiers...His message was clear and well received: 1) He was proud to be an

---

153. Rachel Zimmerman, "Locke pays a visit to China's bustling, cosmopolitan Shanghai," *Seattle Post-Intelligencer*, Oct. 9, 1997

American and proud of his Chinese ancestry; 2) Chinese immigrants helped build the State of Washington and their descendents continue to make significant contributions to the state's diversified economy and cultural life; and 3) Washingtonians benefit today from the flow of goods and services from China, and the people of China could similarly benefit from increased industrial and agricultural products and services from Washington."[154]

Referring to Gov. Locke's home-village visit, Borich wrote,

"...he was accorded a returning hero's welcome. Based on my own experience in China, I believe Governor Locke's visit helped considerably to advance the broad interests of the state."[155]

Borich seemed to have switched from consul work to Council work easily. In that same newsletter, he also talked about the coming October meeting in the U.S. between Chinese President Jiang Zemin and President Clinton and important bilateral issues to watch, such as China's accession to the WTO, nonproliferation, Tiananmen sanctions, trade and Taiwan. He then informed the members of his invitation to Gov. Locke to brief the Council on the China trip at a luncheon, his own scheduled speech at the World Trade Center Tacoma on Hong Kong's economy since handover, the outlook of privatization of China's state-run firms, the results of Gov. Locke's trip to China, and Jiang Zemin's visit. He even welcomed new members into the Council.

But Borich was also so modest. In the beginning of that newsletter, he said he was endeavoring to fill the very large pair of shoes left behind by Eden Woon.

Whether or not Woon would agree about those shoes, there were certainly very large issues for Borich to follow. In mid-1997, the Asian financial crisis hit. Not only did it send currencies and stocks tumbling across Asia, it was also affecting the American economy. For months, China had stayed calm in the storm and had not devalued its currency, the yuan. But the temptation was there. Would it devalue or would it not? Borich had been watching. He talked to the press about it and expressed his hope that China would not devalue yuan. For if China did, Washington state's exporters were sure to be hurt.

---

154. Washington State China Relations Council archives.
155. Ibid.

To the delight of Borich and everyone involved in China trade, China stayed firm throughout the crisis and resisted a devaluation of the yuan. For that, China won praise around the world.

In April 1998, Borich had invited the American Ambassador to China, former Sen. James Sasser, to be the keynote speaker at the Council's annual banquet. Ambassador Sasser talked about how U.S. relations with China had come far over the two years since his appointment. He also praised China's leadership in the midst of Asia's gut-wrenching economic crisis by providing money to help bail out the Thai economy and keeping China's currency stable.[156]

By not devaluing its currency, China also helped to prevent serious damage to Hong Kong's economy. With the coming anniversary of Hong Kong's handover, how was Hong Kong doing in its first year as a special administrative region of China? It was a topic of interest to many of Washington state's businesses.

Therefore, in June 1998, the Council co-sponsored a national conference in Seattle named "Hong Kong One Year After Transition: Business Opportunities & Policy Challenges," together with the New York-based Asia Society and the Hong Kong Trade Development Council.[157]

More than 200 China experts, business leaders and government officials attended the conference. Chief Secretary of Hong Kong, Anson Chan, was a keynote speaker. Her message was that China's leaders had honored their promise to give Hong Kong people a high degree of autonomy; it was the fate of China's MFN in the U.S. Congress that had Hong Kong worried. She urged U.S. lawmakers to consider the impact of their actions not just on China, but on Hong Kong and a region already reeling from the Asian economic crisis.[158] She gave some figures:

"Should the U.S. revoke MFN trading status for the mainland of China, Hong Kong would suffer as a direct result of the reduction in trade

---

156. Imbert Matthee, "Ambassador To China Sees Warming Signs," *Seattle Post-Intelligencer*, Apr. 4, 1998, p. A2
157. Imbert Matthee, "Little Change Seen In Hong Kong After Takeover By China," *Seattle Post-Intelligencer*, Mar. 9, 1998, p. A2
158. Ron Redmond, "China's Governing Of Hong Kong Gets Some High Marks," *Seattle Post-Intelligencer*, Jun. 16, 1998, p. A1

flows…There would be a loss of income of around $3.2 billion to $4.5 billion and around 61,000 to 87,000 jobs."[159]

Borich understood the significance of MFN to Hong Kong. He also understood Hong Kong's significance to the whole of China. He commented during the conference:

> "Hong Kong does not exist in a vacuum…Its impact on China has been going on for 15 or 20 years. It's primarily economic in nature, but there are also a lot of other spinoffs from this economic fusion. You can see it in the rising expectations and rising living standards throughout southeastern China. Fifty years down the road, I think it will be more a case of China resembling Hong Kong than of Hong Kong resembling China."[160]

But before China resembled Hong Kong, Borich saw something going on in China that resembled Taiwan—the village committee elections.

With the experiment started in early 1980s and the village election law adopted in 1987, by the end of 1998, 90% of China's 1 million villages had already held elections. Borich was very optimistic about those elections, he told a local paper:

> "In Taiwan, it was an experiment, too, when it started out. Not to put too fine a point on the parallels, but in the late '50s and early '60s, Taiwan did the same thing at the village level. They began at the village level and moved up to the counties."[161]

There was something else that made Borich and all Seattleites optimistic in the spring of 1999. Seattle had been chosen out of 40 U.S. cities to host the next World Trade Organization meeting. Borich had been following closely China's progress on its WTO accession. He was hoping that China would be able to clear all hurdles by the time of the Seattle Round of the WTO in November 1999. Absent WTO membership, he said,

159. Ibid.
160. Ron Redmond, "Hong Kong Revisited A Year After Takeover Top Official Will Keynote Seattle Talk," *Seattle Post-Intelligencer*, Jun. 15, 1998, p. C1
161. Ron Redmond, "Village Elections Can Lead To Major Changes In China," *Seattle Post-Intelligencer*, Dec. 14, 1998, p. A2

"China must win annual renewal of Most Favored Nation trade status by Congress. This hangs over trade because it leaves tariff levels up in the air."[162]

In the meanwhile, Washington state was doing fine in its China trade. The previous year, 1998, saw $3.6 billion in Washington goods moved to China, making China Washington's third largest importer. In the same year, China sent $8.4 billion of exports to or through Seattle.[163]

In early April, Chinese Premier Zhu Rongji was in the U.S. to meet President Clinton over a number of tough issues, from human rights to China's WTO accession; from the growing trade imbalance to accusations of China's theft of U.S. nuclear secrets.

Comparing the national and the local scene, Borich, who had just returned from a 12-day China trip promoting business and cultural exchanges between Washington state and China, said:

> "The bandwidth tends to be a bit longer in sub-national relations...Whatever the differences with Washington, D.C., there seems to be a lot of interest and action at developing grass-roots relationships. We tend to be more practical and less polemic in our dealings with China."[164]

When U.S. and Chinese negotiators agreed on China's concessions for entering the WTO, Borich had one word, "Breathtaking."[165] In the end, however, Clinton turned Chinese Premier Zhu Rongji down. Borich was disappointed. But he kept his hopes high.

On April 19, at a luncheon in Seattle sponsored by Cosco (China Ocean Shipping Company) celebrating 20 years of trade between the U.S. and China and attended by Chinese Ambassador Li Zhaoxing, Sen. Patty Murray, and Robert

---

162. Glenn R. Rascall, "Banana, China and politics on WTO agenda," *Puget Sound Business Journal*, Mar. 26, 1999
163. Stephen H. Dunphy, "All Over But The Shouting," *The Seattle Times*, Dec. 26, 1999
164. Stephan H. Dunphy, "Washington And China Get Along Fine," *The Seattle Times*, Apr. 4, 1999
165. Bruce Ramsey, "China's admittance to WTO: It will be a close call," *Seattle Post-Intelligencer*, Sept. 27, 1999

Kapp, now President of the US-China Business Council, Borich talked about the bilateral agreement:

> "I don't think there's that much distance between the two sides. My anticipation is that they may come to a conclusion in the next couple of weeks. The more difficult step will be for congress to modify the Jackson-Vanik Amendment to allow for China to have permanent normal trading status. Under the best of circumstances, it's going to be a difficult fight, but not an impossible one."[166]

Borich was also right about the difference between national and sub-national relations. Even though Premier Zhu didn't get what he had come for—a U.S.-China bilateral agreement on WTO—Washington state got a number of agreements it wanted. One was a breakthrough after years of waiting: the ending of a ban by China on wheat from the Pacific Northwest. Another was to increase flights and permit additional air carriers between the U.S. and China.[167]

In early May, at a Seattle forum co-sponsored by the Council and the Asia Society, Borich and other experts talked about China's chance of joining the WTO in 1999, the Congress, and possible fresh demonstrations and crackdowns on the 10th anniversary of that June 4th event.

But it was not to be June 4th that would give our trade advocates headaches. On May 8, 1999, U.S.-led NATO bombed the Chinese embassy in Yugoslavia, an action the U.S. government claimed was a mistake. The Chinese government condemned it. 100,000 Beijingers protested in front of the American embassy, breaking windows and doors. Although President Clinton apologized and U.S. government also agreed to pay for the property loss, damage had been done. The U.S. and China reduced the level of diplomatic contact for about four months.[168]

But Borich had kept in touch with the Chinese officials after the incident. Within a week, he informed the public that Beijing desired no retreat in bilateral commercial relations and to continue all programs and planned events.[169]

---

166. Bruce Ramsey, "Optimism for China in the WTO," *Seattle Post-Intelligencer*, Apr. 20, 1999

167. Stephan H. Dunphy, "Economic Memo," *The Seattle Times*, Apr. 18, 1999

168. BBC News, "On This Day—May 9, 1999," http://news.bbc.co.uk/onthisday/hi/dates/stories/may/9/newsid_2519000/2519271.stm

169. Steve Dunphy, "The Newsletter," *The Seattle Times,* May 14, 1999

Later that month, in the Council newsletter, Borich suggested that members stick with their plans in China, but keep a low profile:

> "My general advice at this point is that what happened in Belgrade and China should not cause you to change or abandon your basic business plans and strategy for doing business in China. The fundamental economic dynamic between China and the U.S. has not changed, nor, in their own self-interest, will the Chinese seek to change it."[170]

Borich stuck to Council plans, too, which included receiving a Jiangsu Province delegation visiting Seattle in late May and a Washington State delegation visit to China's northeast in early July.

With a grant earlier that year from the Foundation for Russian American Economic Cooperation, Borich had been working on the feasibility study on a project called the East by West Corridor. The idea was to have empty cargo containers that had carried U.S. goods to the Russian Far East sent to northeast China to be refilled with Chinese products, then sent to the Russian port at Vladivostok for transshipment to Seattle and Tacoma.[171]

As part of the project, Borich and a 15-member group, headed by Washington's Secretary of State Ralph Munro and with members of Port of Tacoma and Port of Everett, visited Vladivostok as well as Heilongjiang and Jilin, two Chinese northeast provinces across the border from Russia. The three sides, Americans, Chinese and Russians, signed a protocol promising to open the border to goods to and from North America. It was a great trip, Borich told me later.

That July, however, also saw a new dispute between China and Taiwan. Taiwan President Lee Teng-hui had come up with a theory of "state-to-state" relationship between Taiwan and China and talked about Taiwan being a sovereign and independent state. China reacted angrily with threats. Would the war of words escalate? Borich, the only Taiwan hand among the Council directors, said calmly,

---

170. Washington State China Relations Council, *"China Update,"* Vol. 1, Iss. V, May 1999
171. Bruce Ramsey, "A China-Seattle trade route, via Russia, is in the works," *Seattle Post-Intelligencer,* Jul. 5, 1999

"...as long as things are kept in the realm of statements, and the rest of the world does not change their policies in respect to 'one China,' my guess is that Beijing's response will remain verbal."[172]

If the bombing incident and the Taiwan dispute were frustrating, there was something encouraging. If his predecessors had to worry about the annual MFN debate in Congress, Borich could look forward to China's WTO membership and the end of the annual debate.

On November 15, 1999, US-China Bilateral Market Access Agreement was signed. And it was signed before the WTO meeting in Seattle as many had hoped. Borich talked to the media the next day. With China in the WTO, Borich said,

"...important new markets will open for our products and services. It will be a huge boost for our manufacturing, financial and agriculture sectors as various aspects of the agreement are phased in."[173]

Borich had a Council conference organized within a few days. The speakers included Wang Yunxiang, China's consul general in San Francisco; Sidney Rittenberg, the legendary consultant who had lived in China for many years; and Pitman Potter, a China specialist at the University of British Columbia. Everyone was excited about the agreement. Yes, the deal had been signed, but it didn't mean that Washington state businesses or American businesses were ready to benefit from all the market concessions negotiated by the U.S. with China upon China's accession. As Borich said:

"...the deal signed last week does not have to be ratified. But it includes permanent normal trading status which does require a vote of both houses of Congress..."

"Voting down normal trade status would mean that all other WTO members would get the benefit of China's concessions, and the United States would not."[174]

---

172. Bruce Ramsey, "China experts hope its just 'war of words,'" *Seattle Post-Intelligencer*, Jul. 17, 1999

173. Arthur C. Gorlick, "State's products may pour into China, which means 'jobs, jobs, jobs,'" *Seattle Post-Intelligencer*, Nov. 16, 1999

174. Bruce Ramsey, "Trade with China will eventually normalize, analysts say," *Seattle Post-Intelligencer*, Nov. 20, 1999

Later that month, when the Chinese delegation headed by Shi Guangsheng, China's minister of Foreign Trade and Economic Cooperation, arrived in Seattle for the Third WTO Ministerial Conference scheduled from November 30 to December 3, the Council and the US-China Business Council jointly gave a reception.

However, during the Ministerial, more than 50,000 people[175] filled downtown Seattle protesting it. With the demonstration turning into a riot, the meeting was shut down. The so-called Millennium Round came to be remembered as the Battle of Seattle. And it was fought in Washington of all places, the most trade dependent state in the union.

No matter what the Battle of Seattle meant, it inaugurated the new century for Washington state trade and the Washington State China Relations Council. It looked messy and difficult. But Borich, our turn-of-the-century-director, was ready to take it on. Taking it on with him was Donald E. Miller, Council president for 2000–01 and CEO/owner of Ederer Inc.

Borich stayed focused on China's trade status. As the new bilateral agreement required U.S. Congress to grant China permanent normal trade relations (PNTR) to replace MFN, a battle was now expected in the other Washington. It was to be no less fierce (though certainly less physical) than the Battle of Seattle. Borich gave his view this way:

> "China will gain entry into the WTO whether the U.S. approves normal trade-relations status or not. It's not a vote against China. It's a vote against U.S. businesses, U.S. farmers and U.S. workers....the China issue is more about access to the market for the U.S. than the other way around."[176]

Borich knew how PNTR for China would benefit Washington state, from Boeing to Starbucks, from wheat to apples, from Washington-Sichuan and Seattle-Chonging sister relations to Seattle-Shanghai and Tacoma-Tianjin friendship port relations.

---

175. Heath Foster and Kery Murakami, "Schell And Stamper Can Expect To Be Severely Criticized," *Seattle Post-Intelligencer*, Dec. 4, 1999, p. A6
176. Stephan H. Dunphy, "All Over But The Shouting," *The Seattle Times*, Dec. 26, 1999

In early March of 2000, Borich became part of an ad hoc committee to coordinate lobbying and education in support of PNTR. Heading the group was Patricia Davis, President of WCIT. Other members included leaders of the state Department of Community, Trade and Economic Development and the U.S. Export Assistance Center.

Late that month, Borich was in China on a trade mission sponsored jointly by the Council and the Trade Development Alliance of Greater Seattle. The purpose of the trip was to promote better trade relations between the Puget Sound area and cities in the Yangtze River area. As the former Shanghai consul general overseeing consular affairs in the east China region, everywhere the delegation went, from Shanghai to Nanjing, everyone knew Borich.[177] One could imagine how Borich felt back in his old stomping ground. In the Council newsletter that month, Borich wrote about his new and old impression of Shanghai,

> "In my inaugural speech as consul general six years ago in Shanghai, I remarked: 'In economic development, all of China looks to Shanghai.' Those words remain true today. Shanghai is still China's economic powerhouse."[178]

In Chengdu, a Washington State and Sichuan Province friendship association agreement was signed,[179] providing a new mechanism for contacts between Washington and Sichuan. Seeing China's economy steadily growing after the Asian financial crisis and thinking of the coming battle in Congress at home, Borich said,

> "...the real danger to the U.S. is not posed by a China that succeeds economically, but rather by one that fails."[180]

On May 24, 2000, the good news came that the House voted to grant PNTR to China. On September 19, the Senate approved the bill H.R. 4444 granting the same. And on October 10, President Clinton signed the bill into law, terminating the practice of annual review of China's MFN based on the 1974 Trade Act, and establishing permanent normal trade relations with China upon its entry into the WTO.

---

177. Stephen H. Dunphy, "The News Letter," *The Seattle Times*, Mar. 24, 2000
178. Washington State China Relations Council, "*China Update*," Vol. 2, Iss. IV, Apr. 2000
179. Stephen H. Dunphy, "The News Letter," *The Seattle Times*, Mar. 30, 2000
180. Seattle Times, Economic Memo, "A Mission to China," Mar. 19, 2000

What a year!

January 2001 started the George W. Bush administration. The agricultural subsidy issues still being negotiated between China and US and Europe, however, were holding back China's WTO accession.

In terms of U.S.-China relations, however, it was as the Chinese saying went, "hardly has one wave subsided when another rises." With the U.S. payment just made in the beginning of the year for the 1999 bombing of Chinese embassy in Yugoslavia, a new crisis rose: the spy plane incident over the South China Sea, in which one Chinese fighter crashed and an American surveillance plane made an emergency landing in Hainan, China. It all happened on April 1.

The standoff lasted about 11 days before the American crew was freed. But the plane was still in Hainan, with tough negotiations ahead. Borich, however, didn't seem worried. He told a local paper:

> "I think this incident has caused some strain on the relationship, but I don't think it's terribly serious. I think it's transitory."[181]

Within three weeks of the incident, Borich organized a timely Council luncheon with the theme "U.S.-China relations under the Bush administration." The speaker was Darryl Johnson, deputy assistant secretary of state for East Asian and Pacific affairs, a friend, and a former colleague of Borich's, and a man in the know. Mr. Johnson told Council members about the talks in Beijing over the return of the plane and described them as "businesslike but difficult."[182] He expected that there would be more meetings and hoped that the issue would be solved in a way that would further U.S.-China relations.

In early May, Borich organized another Council event, this time an afternoon tea with none other than the new Chinese Ambassador Yang Jiechi. Mr. Yang talked not only about the spy plane incident, but also other issues of dispute between U.S. and China, such as the U.S. missile defense system, and President Bush's plan for the largest weapons sales to date to Taiwan. Mr. Yang went on to say:

---

181. Marni Leff, "U.S.-China trade not hurt by standoff, experts say," *Seattle Post-Intelligencer*, Apr. 12, 2001

182. Martin Fackler, "U.S. says China will now discuss return of plane," *Seattle Post-Intelligencer*, Apr. 19, 2001

"When the Cold War is over, to adopt Cold War mentality or to continue to maintain that kind of mentality in treating China will be a very dangerous path...A prosperous China will be a plus for the United States, a weak, divided China would really be a threat."[183]

Ambassador Yang's views seemed to be in agreement with that of Borich's. Borich stayed optimistic over the spy plane talks. With the Asia Pacific Cities Summit to convene in Seattle on May 6–8 and with 90 cities to be represented, Borich said he didn't think the tension between China and the U.S. over the spy plane would impact participation by Chinese cities.[184] He was right. A dozen Chinese cities arrived for the meeting, including Chonqing, Seattle's sister city.[185]

Not only did they arrive in Seattle, they also arrived at Borich's home. Even though the Council was not the lead organization in the event, Borich and his wife Hsiao-hui invited heads of Chinese delegations to a private reception, in the Borich backyard. It was a nice day, Borich said, with 40–50 guests, Chinese and American. The food was a mix, too, Chinese and American.

August was the Council's annual banquet time. Borich had a very distinguished and surprise guest for the occasion: Ambassador Joseph W. Prueher, who had just completed a successful career highlighted by his vital role in ending the spy plane standoff. As the former Commander-in-Chief of the U.S. Pacific Command (CINCPAC), Ambassador Prueher had really been the right man in the right place at the right time when the spy plane incident happened. Council members had a treat in the ambassador's speech on the drama of U.S.-China relations around the incident, and from a real insider during those negotiations.

Borich was very proud when he told me about the "trifecta" of events that had come together in the aftermath of the spy plane incident. But they didn't "just happen" as he described. They happened because of Borich's connections, reputation, and quick work.

---

183. Paul Nyhan, "Chinese envoy strike a moderate tone," *Seattle Post-Intelligencer*, May 5, 2001
184. Stephen Dunphy, "The Newsletter," *The Seattle Times*, Apr. 24, 2001
185. Jim Brunner, "Peaceful protesters greet global city summit," *The Seattle Times*, May 7, 2001

Suddenly, out of the blue, September 11, 2001, brought probably the darkest moment of the new 21st century for America. The tragedy and anger soon mobilized a new coalition in the war against terror.

If there was any thing positive that came out of 9/11, it had to be the improvement of U.S.-China relations. Chinese President Jiang Zemin was one of the first world leaders to call President Bush to offer condolences and support for America.

President Bush, recognizing the importance in America's suddenly renewed relations with China, traveled to Shanghai a little over a month after 9/11 to attend the APEC 2001 Leaders Meeting, from October 15–21. There President Bush and President Jiang gave a joint press conference. If one had wondered about the post-9/11 U.S.-China relationship, President Bush's remarks cleared it all up:

> "President Jiang and the government stand side by side with the American people as we fight this evil force. China is a great power. And America wants a constructive relationship with China."[186]

Contrasting the dark September 11, November 11, 2001, was a red-letter day. News broke out from Doha, Qatar that trade ministers from across the world had approved China's entry into the WTO. China's membership was to be official 30 days later. It finally came after fifteen years of negotiations, two years after the U.S.-China bilateral agreement, and many heads of hair turned gray, as then Chinese Premier Zhu Rongji commented.

Borich cheered in the December newsletter:

> "'CHINA JOINS THE WTO'
>
> On December 11, China officially became the 143rd member of the World Trade Organization. On December 27, President Bush made a formal proclamation conferring permanent normal trade status on China, thus ending for China the Jackson-Vanik requirement of an annual extension of China's normal trade status."[187]

---

186. http://www.sinomania.com/CHINANEWS/bush-zemin_press_conference_in_shanghai.htm
187. Washington State China Relations Council, *"China Update,"* Vol. 3, Iss. XII, Dec. 2001

He then went on to explain some of the changes to take effect immediately, such as tariffs on auto imports and foreign agricultural products.

It is not hard to imagine how Washington state's China trade community embraced the news. It is also easy to guess what a joyous time it must have been for the Council. Who could forget how in earlier years the Council directors and members had to lobby hard each year for China's MFN? Who could forget the sad and low days of the Council in the aftermath of Tiananmen?

With China in the WTO, 2002 looked and felt great. Borich filled the Council calendar with events. Just to read the schedules through the first half of that year makes one feel busy.

Jan. 8: Networking breakfast on "China's Growing Wireless Industry."

Jan. 24: Members Forum: "Success in South China."

Feb. 5: WSCRC Spring Festival Party, partnering with Washington State-Sichuan Friendship Association in raising funds to build a primary school in Sichuan.

Feb. 22: First of two programs on China's entry to the World Trade Organization and what that would mean for the region's business interests, U.S. national security and China itself. Guest speaker: Wang Yunxiang, China's consul-general to the Northwest.

Apr. 2: WSCRC and the Trade Development Alliance of Greater Seattle: "97 Plus 5 Equals 2002: Hong Kong and the U.S. Five Years after the Hand-Over," featuring Michael Klosson, U.S. consul general to Hong Kong.

May 16: "Opportunity and Regulatory Changes in Post-WTO China."

May 30: "China's Potential—The Views of International Money Managers."

June 20: "Distinguished Speaker Series: On Hong Kong." Speaker: Jacqueline Ann Willis, Hong Kong commissioner for economic and trade affairs, on Hong Kong's future and China's accession to the WTO.[188]

---

188. Seattle Post-Intelligencer, "Local business calendar," 2002

And on June 27, Deputy United States Trade Representative John M. Huntsman spoke at the Council's annual banquet. Besides commenting on China's WTO membership and its new challenges ahead, Mr. Huntsman praised the leading role that Washington state companies played in energizing commercial relations with China and in bringing about the passing in congress of PNTR.[189] He mentioned Boeing, Weyerhaeuser, Microsoft and Starbucks. All of them were long-time Council members.

As a foreign economic advisor to Chongqing since 1998,[190] Borich had also been following developments around Chongqing's new provincial level municipality status granted a few years back and the "Go West" drive China had launched in 2000 to develop the country's western provinces including Sichuan. With the 20th anniversary of both Washington-Sichuan sister-state relations and Seattle-Chongqing sister-city relations coming up back to back, Borich had also traveled to Chongqing that spring.

With China's central government planning to invest $200 billion in Chongqing, Borich said he believed that like Shanghai was to eastern China in the '90s and Guangzhou/Shenzhen to southeastern China in the '80s, Chongqing was expected to play the leading role in the rapid development of western China in the current decade.[191]

If the new decade had new expectations for Chongqing, it seemed to pose new challenges to the Council.

In fact, 2001–02 turned out to be a "difficult period" for the Council, as Borich put it. Council membership and revenues had been dropping. Borich had been thinking about possible causes. The first one, he believed, was the 9/11 terrorist attacks and the slumping economy afterwards, especially from the effect of globally reduced air travel and of the "dot-gone" bust after the surge in Internet related businesses in the late 1990s. But he also detected another cause: the pas-

---

189. Washington State China Relations Council, "*China Update*," Vol. 4, Iss. VI, Jul. 2002

190. Trade Development Alliance, "Chongqing City Report," http://www.cityofseattle.net/tda/trade_info/TBfrontsisterchongqing.htm

191. Stephen Dunphy, "The Newsletter," *The Seattle Times*, May 8, 2002

sage of PNTR by Congress and China's entry into the WTO. He pointed out that there was a mistaken impression gaining popularity that:

> "...the big issues in U.S.-China relations are behind us and organizations like the Washington State China Relations Council are no longer as relevant as they once were."[192]

Serving as the Council president that year was Andrea B. Riniker, executive director of the Port of Tacoma. To tackle the new challenges, Riniker called an unusual Saturday session of the board of directors on September 28. It was a "watershed meeting for the Council," in Borich's words, a meeting called to consider redefining the Council's mission, priorities and work plan for the coming year and beyond. Borich devoted a special newsletter to the meeting. After reaffirming the mission of the Council, he wrote:

> "Convinced that there still remains an important role for the Council to play in the region's interactions with China...The consensus was that the Council's top priority should be service to its members, with service to the State of Washington as the second priority."[193]

With the priorities set, the work plan for 2003 included a number of new initiatives to build membership and provide new sources of revenue. They included broadening the business counseling services for members and as a tool to recruit new members; expanding the distinguished speakers program; creating a trade show each spring with Chinese buyers or vendors; and organizing a sector-specific China mission each fall.[194]

On the shift of emphasis to commercial programs, Borich explained,

> "Our resources will be primarily focused on member services with our orientation more toward commercial relations and somewhat less toward cultural and academic ties. However, we will not abandon the cultural and academic interests of this state vis a vis China; instead, we will support other organizations

---

192. Stephen H. Dunphy, "Transformation of a city: Chongqing getting $200 billion infusion," *The Seattle Times*, Nov. 16, 2002
193. Washington State China Relations Council, "*China Update*," Vol. 4, Iss. IX, Sept. 2002
194. Ibid.

whose primary goals fall within these areas rather than taking the lead ourselves as we have often done in the past."[195]

To the media, Borich said:

"Both the times and the interests of most of our members dictate that we specialize in providing more of the services that they need and want, as they pursue their business interests in China."[196]

The Council, Borich also told them, had identified two key areas of interest for the new initiatives: environmental business opportunities with China and the Beijing Olympics in 2008. An environmental seminar had already been planned for spring 2003, expecting Chinese and Northwest officials, businesses and experts.[197]

As he expressed, it was now his personal goal to keep the Council healthy by ensuring that it remained an organization serving its members' interests, Borich didn't wait to start the new initiatives.

In October 2002, there was a Council breakfast roundtable on "International Ocean Shipping in a Deregulated Environment." In November, it was a seminar on "Howdy Partner—Strategies for Getting Your Business Partner to Seattle." In December, there was a luncheon on "China and the WTO: New Opportunities or New Challenges."[198]

2003 saw more clearly the new emphasis of Council programs on specific industries, services, or opportunities. For instance, the "Environmental Conference" on major hazardous-waste treatment projects and technologies in the hazardous-waste treatment field; the seminar on enterprise strategy titled "Special Delivery;" and the talk on "Business Opportunities with Yangzhou, China."[199]

---

195. Ibid.

196. Steve Wilhelm, "China relations council looks in new directions," *Puget Sound Business Journal,* Nov. 1, 2002

197. Stephen H. Dunphy, "Transformation of a city: Chongqing getting $200 billion infusion," *The Seattle Times,* Nov. 16, 2002

198. Seattle Post-Intelligencer, "Business calendar," 2002

199. Seattle Post-Intelligencer, "Business calendar," 2003

In October 2003, Borich helped organize and joined Governor Locke's third trade mission to China. In Beijing, Shanghai and Guangzhou, the delegation pushed everything from printing presses to potatoes, from Boeing jetliners to Starbucks coffee. Meeting with the 2008 Beijing Olympic Games organizers, they also promoted Washington companies that could provide engineering, architecture and other expertise for staging the Games.[200] It was a successful mission with tangible results in millions of dollars in actual sales and projected sales in 12 months.[201]

However, with the steady growth of U.S.-China trade over the years, there was also a steadily growing problem: the U.S. trade deficit with China. In 2003, that deficit was $124 billion.[202] The situation of Washington state-China trade was similar. The two-way trade that year grew to $16.9 billion, but with Washington imports accounting for $13.9 billion[203] of the total. Borich began to talk about the issue with the media. When U.S. deficits with Japan started growing rapidly in the 1980s, Borich said, relations between the two soured. He feared that could happen again with China.[204]

But trade deficit could wait. Something else couldn't. The 25th anniversary of the Council was coming. It was party time!

On the evening of June 18, 2004, after a great deal of preparation, Borich opened the gala celebrating the 25th anniversary of the Washington State China Relations Council at the Bell Harbor International Conference Center in Seattle. United States Ambassador to China Clark T. Randt Jr. was the keynote speaker. Ambassador Peng Keyu, Chinese consul general in San Francisco, read a congratulatory letter from China's Foreign Minister Li Zhaoxing. Ms. Starr M. Tavenner, the Council president in 2004 and director of China programs of Boeing, gave her remarks. Sponsoring the evening were long-term outstanding and sus-

---

200. MATR News, "Deals signed during Locke's China trip," Oct. 15, 2003, http://www.matr.net/article-8413.html

201. WSDA news release, "Gov. Gary Locke Declares China/Vietnam Trade Mission Huge Success," Sept. 27, 2004

202. The US-China Business Council, http://www.uschina.org/statistics/2004balanceoftrade.html

203. Washington State Department of Community, Trade & Economic Development

204. Stephen Dunphy, "Trade deficit with China coming into focus," *The Seattle Times*, Sept. 17, 2003

taining member firms of the Council including The Boeing Company, Citifor Incorporated, Expeditors International, Garvey Schubert and Barer, the Port of Seattle, the Port of Tacoma and Russell Investment Group. Attending the celebration were Council founders, including Mr. Robert Anderson, Ms. Patricia Baillargeon, Mr. Stanley Barer, former directors, including Mr. Robert Kapp, Mr. William Abnett, and representatives of member firms and organizations, as well as families and friends.

Listening to the distinguished speakers, enjoying an elegant dinner, the celebrants were also treated to a slide show of 25 years of the Washington State-China relationship. It was heart-warming to see those enlarged stills of Deng Xiaoping and the Liu Lin Hai in Seattle in 1979.

The gala was also Borich's favorite event, as he told me later. I bet it was also Borich's proudest moment as the executive director of the Council.

The Seattle Times carried a special column on the event afterward titled "China ties started early, stayed strong." It mentioned the Council founders, commented on their vision 25 years earlier, and quoted Borich:

> "Few could have imagined where China would be now. You really had to have a vivid imagination to see where trade would go in 25 years."[205]

Vivid imagination indeed. It was that imagination that gave the Council its birth. It was that imagination that led the Council to its 25th birthday. With the same imagination, Borich was determined to continue taking the Council forward and beyond.

Now five years into the 21st century, the Council is no longer the Council of the 1980s or 1990s, at least in four areas.

One: the newsletter. What used to be printed on paper and snail-mailed under Kapp, Abnett, and Woon had gone electronic under Borich since 1999. The newsletter, a monthly to bimonthly, is called "China Update," reminding one of the annual China Trade Update conference started by Kapp. Former China for-

---

205. Stephen Dunphy, "China ties started early, stayed strong," *The Seattle Times*, Jun. 20, 2004

eign policy executive that he was, Borich has put more China analysis into the newsletter, the way he preferred, and less account of Council events. It is also available to non-members, for a fee.

Two: consulting. Continuing in the spirit of the new initiatives from late 2002, the Council started a new consulting program in early 2005. With the newly formed Consulting Services Group composed of member companies with expertise in various fields related to China business, the Council offers an initial consultation to member clients with their China business aims, concerns and questions. The client then decides to engage or not any of the participating firms. The service is offered to non-members, too, for a fee.

In fact, it was for the consulting program that Borich went to China in early June and returned with a memorandum of agreement with the Chinese Entrepreneur Survey System. CESS is a unit within the Development Research Center of the State Council and an association of 19,000 Chinese companies. Borich sees CESS as a great partner in helping Council members and their clients develop their business in China in the future.

To debut in October 2005 is another new service-oriented program called "China Business Planner." A half-day yearly program with special emphasis on sectors important to Washington state—IT, environmental technology, health care, biotechnology, aerospace, and agriculture—it will help members and other participants plan their China business for the following year. It will also address China WTO-related issues, business issues such as international and inland transportation and human resources, and pending regulatory and legal changes in the U.S. and China that would impact bilateral business.

Three: staff. For the first time the Council has a Deputy Director, R. Scott Heinlein, in charge of programs and membership. Beginning as program manager in 2000, not only did the capable Scott take on the unprecedented title a year later, he had also joined the Council in a different way. With a degree in Chinese studies, Heinlein had "defected" from the Foundation for Russian American Economic Cooperation, and recommended himself to the Council. He succeeded, and has been Borich's deputy since.

Four: logo. With the reign of Borich, the Council also adopted a new logo. On the horizontal English name of the Council, a stylish red vertical seal forms the background of Chinese characters of "Washington China Exchange." Contributing to the design: Mrs. Borich!

Busy with preparation for the Council's 2005 banquet in early June, not to say with a schedule of three speeches a month and three trips to China a year on average, Borich let me squeeze in an interview one morning. As I had long awaited, I finally got to ask him some "tough questions," after checking with him some of the events and programs first.

Having worked for years on both sides of the Taiwan Strait, did he ever have any, even a little bit, preference for the Chinese on either side?

A true diplomat that he was once, Borich gave me a quick lesson on how a diplomat should never forget that he or she was not serving the client country, but his or her own country. No matter whether it was the Taiwan desk or the China desk, he said, he had always worked on the American desk.

Having worked as a consul general with a staff of 150, was the Council work perhaps too easy, a case of "big material put to small use," as the Chinese say?

No, but different, Borich said. With 150 people under him, he was not directly responsible for all the consulate work. But with 150 members, each needed to feel directly "touched" by the Council.

What about budget? As consul general, he never had to worry, I said. Borich replied, he did learn to do things that were once outside his comfort zone. But he liked the challenge. After eight years, he said, he was still having fun. I guess that is the most important thing—having fun.

Very soon, I said, you are going to outdo Mr. Kapp as the longest-serving director. Borich laughed, and said he was sure he wouldn't be around for the 50th anniversary. Now I laughed and said, I am sure you would be for the 30th!

I came away from the interview pretty satisfied until I realized I had to ask Borich one more thing. As the current and on-going executive director, would he give a five-year prediction of the Council? I emailed Borich my last question.

Borich emailed back. His answer, as follows, is in fact an outline of the Council in the near future to come:

> "I think that the Council's basic role—assisting our members and promoting commercial, cultural and academic ties between Washington and China—will remain the same. However, our consulting work could provide both greater size and resources for the Council. If our consulting work is successful, I envision the Consulting Services Group as eventually forming a for-profit subsidiary of the WSCRC and providing significant support to our basic mission."

I wish Borich more fun and the Washington State China Relations Council further success!

Joseph J. Borich, 2005

Part III

Presiding

Introduction

If the founders of the Council were visionary architects and the directors were knowledgeable managers, the presidents of the Washington State China Relations Council had to be the all-seeing superintendents. As the head of the executive committee, a president had to take the lead in making sure the Council was going in the right direction, with right programs to offer, with a stable membership, with sound sources of financing, with good community response, and with good results of its work in Washington state-China relations. A president, for many years, was also the author of Council's annual report.

With all the responsibilities at the Council, one should not forget that our presidents have all had their very high-level day jobs. They have been CEOs, chairmen, presidents, vice presidents and directors of the most prestigious companies or organizations in Washington state.

In its 25-plus years, the Council has had nineteen presidents, with Mr. Robert C. Anderson as the first, Dr. David Bachman as the current, and Mr. William A. Glassford the longest-serving. He served for a total of four one-year terms!

I have tried to reach all presidents, past and the current, and succeeded with many of them. They are still busy with their new businesses, positions, travels or active retirement. I mourn those who have left us forever: Roger N. Christiansen, president for 1981, and Melvin M. Stewart, president for 1987.

Each and every president of the Council has my great respect. But it is beyond my ability to write about their larger-than-Council presidency stories. I have, therefore, asked those I have been able to reach to write a little about their experience as the president of the Council. Fortunately for me, and us, many of them agreed.

In the following pages, after a list of all presidents of the Council over the years, you will find the comments some of them have written most recently, and exclusively, for this book. These comments are truly their words of wisdom—wisdom of leading the Council, and wisdom of developing Washington state-China relations.

3.1

List of Presidents of the Washington State China Relations Council

1980   Robert C. Anderson, Director, Washington State Department of Commerce & Economic Development

1981   Roger N. Christiansen, Senior Vice President, China Development Department, Seattle-First National Bank

1982   James D. Dwyer, Senior Director, Port Development and Relations, Port of Seattle

1983   Stanley H. Barer, Attorney, Garvey, Schubert, Adams & Barer

1984   J. K. Barrington, President, First Interstate Bank of Washington

1985   William E. Franklin, Group Vice President-International, Weyerhaeuser Company

1986   John M. Fluke Jr., Chairman and Chief Executive Officer, John Fluke Manufacturing Company

1987   Melvin M. Stewart, Chairman of the Board, Stevedoring Services of America, Inc.

1988   Richard H. Harding, Senior Vice President, First Interstate Bank of Washington

1989   John M. Swihart, Vice President, International Affairs, The Boeing Company

1990   Timothy C. Herlich, District Sales Manager, Northwest Airlines

1991   William A. Glassford, Senior Vice President, Security Pacific Bank of Washington

1992   Lawrence W. Clarkson, Corporate Vice President, The Boeing Company

1993   Lawrence W. Clarkson, Corporate Vice President, The Boeing Company

1994   Michael E. Bickford, Director of Corporate Positioning, Weyerhaeuser Company

1995   M. R. Dinsmore, Executive Director, Port of Seattle

1996   M. R. Dinsmore, Executive Director, Port of Seattle

1997   William A. Glassford, Senior Vice President, Seafirst Bank

1998   William A. Glassford, Senior Vice President, Seafirst Bank

1999   William A. Glassford, Senior Vice President, Seafirst Bank

2000   Donald E. Miller, Chairman and CEO, Ederer Incorporated

2001   Donald E. Miller, Chairman and CEO, Ederer Incorporated

2002   Andrea B. Riniker, Executive Director, Port of Tacoma

2003   Andrea B. Riniker, Executive Director, Port of Tacoma

2004   Starr M. Tavenner, Director, China Programs, The Boeing Company

2005   David Bachman, Professor, Chair of China Studies Program, Jackson School of International Studies, University of Washington

3.2

In Their Own Words of Wisdom

Robert C. Anderson, President, 1980
(Director, Washington State Department of Commerce & Economic Development; currently Senior Trade Advisor, Snohomish County):

"As the old saying goes 'timing is everything.' The intersection of Deng's visit to Seattle and Gov. Ray's subsequent visit to China prompted Stan Barer and I and the other soon-to-be founding board members to reflect on the impact of emerging China from a political, business and cultural aspect. It became obvious that the short-range and long-range benefits to Washington state were enormous. Stan, from his involvement in securing the COSCO deal and the ensuing dialogue with Chinese officials, and my first-hand observations of China on the ground, prompted the need for a formal vehicle to deal with the complex relationship which was bound to follow.

"The formal organization was really quite easy. Incorporation, initial donors, financial structure, publicity and key sign-off by the political and business community were secured through our personal networks. After appropriate inquiry we approached Bob Kapp to elicit his interest. He agreed and his acceptance further legitimized our endeavor. The deed was done!

"I believe the events of the past 25 plus years, and indeed the most current issues regarding China, justify our vision regarding the relationship. The boards have remained steadfast and the executive leadership, beginning with Bob and carrying foreword to Joe Borich has been superb. What more can we ask? So far so good!"

James D. Dwyer, President, 1982
(Senior Director, Port Development and Relations, Port of Seattle; currently President and CEO, Washington Dental Service):

"Having been one of the founders of the WSCRC and having conceived of the idea during my first trip to China as a member of a delegation from Washington state in 1979, it was an honor to serve as its president in 1982. Among the more satisfying aspects of being associated with the Council was the commitment by its officers and members to a longer-range vision to build an understanding between the people of Washington state and the people of China. While most had a business purpose for membership, there was also a true affection to develop deeper relationships across many areas such as cultural exchanges, the arts and crafts, student exchanges and so forth. The belief was that the better you understood one another, the easier it would be to conduct business. It was also deeply gratifying that the Council became the clear 'go to' source for policy and political recommendations relative to the triangular relationship between Washington state, the federal government and China. The Council was not only not afraid to weigh in on debatable issues, it was proactive and considered a substantive source for business and political advice in Washington state. Of course, the membership fueled the Council, but it was driven always by an immensely dedicated, capable and respected staff."

Stanley H. Barer, President, 1983
(Attorney, Garvey, Schubert, Adams & Barer; currently Of Counsel, Garvey Schubert Barer; Regent, University of Washington; Chairman Emeritus and an owner, Saltchuk Resources, Inc.):

> "It is most gratifying to be one who helped establish and lead the Council in its early years. For over a quarter of a century the Council has been successful. That is because its mission, focus and efforts have been valuable and effective and clearly remain so today. The ever increasing importance of the U.S.-China relationship underscores the future importance and value of the Council."

William E. Franklin, President, 1985
(Group Vice President-International, Weyerhaeuser Company; currently President, Franklin International, Ltd.):

"When I began to remember my time with the Council three thoughts came to mind.

"*First,* the trip to China with Governor Dixie Lee delegation in 1979. What an interesting woman, what an educational experience we all had in Beijing, Chengdu and Shanghai. Meeting men and women there with whom I am still in contact. Watching Mr. Deng Xiaopeng and Dixy interact. He started off huffing and puffing on his cigarette, blowing smoke in her direction, saying, 'China is a *free country,* people are free to do whatever they want.' Puffing more big clouds of smoke in her direction (it was reported he was a three packs a day man). 'I understand in some countries people are not free, some countries even force people who smoke to go into special rooms.' He goes on and on with this charade until Dixy finally gets the joke and realizes someone has told him how intensely she hates smoking and has a big laugh with him at his joke. I thought….what good staff work he has, to know about Dixy's personal habits, and what a sense of humor. Ruth Walsh produced a TV program on the trip entitled '*China: Fourteen Hours Ahead and Fifty Years Behind.*'

"*Second.* Working alongside Bob Kapp, the first executive director of the Council, I observed how one becomes an effective leader to build an outstanding volunteer organization. I was in the process of moving from Hong Kong to Seattle in 1983 when I had a call from Bob saying that the board had asked if I would be a candidate for vice president of the Council. The invitation was presented in a manner that caused me to feel honored and welcome. During the following two years I learned that yes, the board did make these decisions, but Bob had most of the small (and big) details worked out in advance…..what the Japanese call *nemowashi.* And this is exactly how it should work. Most volunteer leaders do not have the time to do the research and analysis to make these decisions. A good executive director does this for them, without taking too much of the personal spotlight, and then invites the board to take ownership and move forward. As I have served with other organizations over the past 20 years Bob Kapp has been my gold standard for executive directors.

"*Third.* In 1984 we commemorated the 200th anniversary of the first trade between China and America. The *Empress of China* set out from New York February 22, 1784, and pulled into Canton on August 28. The ship brought ginseng to China, and returned to New York in the spring of 1785 with tea, silk, porcelain and cotton (and with $30,000 profit on a $120,000 investment). Captain John Green wrote in the ship's log, 'the Chinese never heard of us but we introduced ourselves as a new nation, gave them a description of our country and the importance of trade to advantage of both, which they appear to perfectly understand and wish.' He later wrote 'to the exalted Chinese of the Middle Kingdom between heaven and earth all barbarians were tolerated with equal condescension. The Americans took their place along the other *fanqui*. Because the stars on our flag were mistaken for flowers for a long time all Americans were called "flowery flag devils."' *How China and America, and the world, have changed in the two centuries since 1784. How China and America and the world have changed in the two decades since 1984.*

"I am grateful for the opportunity I had to serve the Washington State China Relations Council."

John M. Fluke, Jr., President, 1986
(Chairman and CEO, John Fluke Manufacturing Company; currently Chairman, Fluke Capital Management, LP):

"In the years I served as volunteer head of the Washington State China Relations Council, the People's Republic of China had taken center stage with the Puget Sound media. Countless conferences were organized around China—from dozens of sister-city relationships to how-to seminars on doing business there—China *was* our future. While there were substantial and legitimate reasons for paying attention to China since relations were normalized in 1979, there had been a number of companies with a history of involvement with China. Fluke Corporation had been selling its products since 1973 and manufacturing product in China for domestic customers since 1979. By the mid-80's, China had become a mega-fad.

"Underneath all the hype and excitement, the substance was nonetheless relentlessly growing. Numerous visits by high-ranking Chinese officials advanced commerce between Northwest companies and a wide variety of China state corporations. The Washington State China Relations Council was the major facilitator of Northwest-China commerce. WSCRC's governance and management were focused on playing this crucial role and did so with impeccable effectiveness. Dr. Robert Kapp was the maestro who orchestrated all the details required to bring high-ranking Chinese officials and Northwest industry leaders together. The result was a symphony played by corporate cash registers for hundreds of businesses.

"Bob was a master at convincing countless delegations of important Chinese decision makers to add Seattle to their itineraries. Northwest business leaders have little time (or patience) for participation in token organizations. But they found real and rewarding value in WSCRC membership. I count myself as very fortunate, indeed, to have served my term under Bob's expert leadership. My good fortune was further multiplied by an excellent executive committee composed of very successful expatriates and experienced international sales and operations managers that populated the managements of their equally successful companies. It was not only a great experience personally, but very rewarding for my company and all of the WSCRC member firms.

"Fluke Corporation can attribute a great deal of credit to the WSCRC for facilitating the opportunity to build lasting relations with many Chinese friends that, in turn, yielded 5% of the company's world-wide business by 1986. There have been many ups and downs in Chinese business levels before and since—but the ups have exceeded the downs over the long term. Today, Danaher Corporation, Fluke Corporation's parent, employs 4,000 people in

China and does over half a billion dollars in sales there—much of it attributable to the many fine people that Danaher inherited when it acquired Fluke in 1998. Linda Cheever has risen from Fluke to a governance role, overseeing all of the China business of Danaher's nearly three dozen divisions.

"Our economic vitality today owes a lot to the critical role the WSCRC played in those years of rapidly expanding commerce between China and the Northwest!"

John M. Swihart, President, 1989
(Vice President, International Affairs, The Boeing Company; currently President, Swihart Consulting, Inc.):

> "In any case I remember that the Council had a lot of activity especially with Boeing actively doing business in China with the aircraft plant in Xi'an. I went to China for a combined Boeing and lecture tour sponsored by the China Trade Association. I lectured on future airplane design work in Shanghai, Beijing and Xi'an. We visited several universities including the Northwestern Polytechnical University in Xi'an, where I met some professors who had graduated from Georgia Tech, which was my alma mater. We also visited the aircraft factories in Shanghai and Beijing. Activity here in Seattle was high because Bob Kapp was such a go-getter and had the businesses and the local government as well as the state government very much interested in pursuing trade with China.

> "I thoroughly enjoyed being President and working to establish more trade with China both for small local business as well as continue to pursue big business for Boeing. We worked on agricultural issues as well."

Timothy C. Herlich, President, 1990
(District Sales Manager, Northwest Airlines):

"1990 was a year in which the Council reached a crossroads in its still-fledgling development. The fall of the U.S.S.R. thrust China into a position of unprecedented political importance. The Tiananmen Square incident of the previous year provided the lightning rod to test this new relationship, and its fallout cast a long, dark shadow on U.S.-China trade relations. The Council's very own viability and existence was at stake for the first time since its inception. The focus of the Council abruptly shifted. Unable to maintain a long-view approach in its trade development activities, the Council embarked on the immediate and pragmatic task of educating and advocating for the retention of Most Favored Nation (MFN) trade status. Executive Director Bill Abnett was exhaustive in carrying out this mission. Unfortunately, Council membership, already feeling the effects of the post-1980s recession, contracted and the organization's financial health was imperiled.

"Amid my grave concerns about the Council's' future, I recall being comforted knowing that we would be able to draw from the expertise of Bill Abnett and my successor, Bill Glassford, to map out a strategic plan for the future. Both Bills were confronted with very difficult decisions to make, personally and professionally, the following year. That the Council endured and is observing its 25th Year is a testament to both of them.

"I was personally gratified to be involved in the initial award and ongoing extension of a travel reward program from my employer at that time, Northwest Airlines. The travel assistance, mandated to support artistic, cultural and educational exchange between Washington state and China under the stewardship of the Council, provided a breadth and depth of interaction which otherwise would have been impossible to conduct.

"Congratulations to the Council and its members for 25-plus years of serving the people of Washington state and China."

Lawrence W. Clarkson, President, 1992, 1993
(Corporate Vice President, The Boeing Company; currently Chairman, Hitco
Carbon Composites, Inc.):

> "During my term as president we had to deal with the reaction to the events in
> Tiananmen Square. Getting approval of MFN for China was a real challenge
> as a result. Bill Abnett resigned for heath reasons as executive director and was
> succeeded by Dr. Robert Kapp. I had a very strong, effective board including
> Bill Glassford, David Tang, Stan Barer, Mic Dismore and Claude Stritmatter
> among others. Program speakers included Michael Bonsignore, CEO of Hon-
> eywell, Sandra Christoff, assistant secretary of State and Ambassador Winston
> Lord."

William A. Glassford, President, 1991, 1997, 1998, 1999
(Senior Vice President, Security Pacific Bank of Washington; Senior Vice President, Seafirst Bank; currently Senior Vice President/International Sales Executive for the Private Bank, Bank of America):

> "Returning after a number of years living in Asia, I reconnected to Seattle through several organizations active in international business. The Washington State China Relations Council was one of these. While the WSCRC was young in life span compared to other Seattle organizations, its strong focus and good leadership allowed it to have a significant presence in the international goings-on in Washington state.

> "I had the pleasure to serve as the president of the Council on two different occasions and, as such, I worked with four different executive directors. Both situations were different, and all four executives had varying styles. My first stint was in 1991-1992. Relations with China and our Council's viability were being constrained by Tiananmen Square issues. Membership and programming revenues had been declining for several years and so we crafted an agreement with the Washington Council on International Trade (WCIT) whereby their executive (and the WSCRC's founding executive), Bob Kapp, took over managing our Council. This resulted in reduced expenses while continuing to have a capable China expert at our helm.

> "As the Council got back on its feet and went back to having its own dedicated executive, I again had an opportunity to serve as president in the 1997-1999 period. The focus for much of this period was the annual China MFN discussions. Today, with China trade so pervasive, it seems amazing that so much time in our country was spent debating whether we should be trading with China at all. The Council endeavored to be a moderating voice. An additional challenge in this period was the change in executives as our able leader, Eden Woon, departed to assume a position in Hong Kong. I recall being in Shanghai with Eden as he introduced me to Joe Borich, then America's consul general in that city. A few months later, Joe became the Council executive director upon retiring from the State Department.

> "Serving as the non-executive president or chairman of a non-profit can be very rewarding. My goal (and hope) has always been to not overly interfere with the executive running the organization unless absolutely required. And, at the Washington State China Relations Council, we have been blessed with great executives who have been skilled in the nuances of our relations with China and with contacts to back these up. For the most part Bill Abnett, Bob Kapp, Eden Woon, and Joe Borich allowed me to stay in the chairman's seat and let them run the show."

Appendix A

Council Classics—Documents of Value

Introduction

The following pages contain a number of documents I selected and find to be the most valuable of the records of and about the Washington State China Relations Council. They include the copy of the original incorporation paper the Council founders filed at the office of the secretary of state in Olympia; four pieces of writing—one from each of the Council directors that is most representative of his time and work at the Council; and the cover of the 25th anniversary gala program, a memorable design.

Events come and events go, but these documents remain. They serve as a testament to the spirit, strength, viability and vitality of the Washington State China Relations Council.

1

Washington State China Relations Council incorporation paper

D291394
FILE NUMBER

DOMESTIC

STATE OF WASHINGTON | DEPARTMENT OF STATE

I, **BRUCE K. CHAPMAN**, Secretary of State of the State of Washington and custodian of its seal, hereby certify that

ARTICLES OF INCORPORATION

of_____WASHINGTON STATE CHINA RELATIONS COUNCIL_____

a domestic corporation of_____Seattle,___Washington,

was filed for record in this office on this date, and I further certify that such Articles remain on file in this office.

In witness whereof I have signed and have affixed the seal of the State of Washington to this certificate at Olympia, the State Capitol,

_____August 6, 1979

BRUCE K. CHAPMAN
SECRETARY OF STATE

ARTICLES OF INCORPORATION

OF

WASHINGTON STATE CHINA RELATIONS COUNCIL

We, the undersigned persons, acting as the incorporators of
a corporation under the provisions of the Washington Nonprofit
Corporation Act (Revised Code of Washington Ch. 24.03), adopt the
following articles of incorporation for such corporation:

ARTICLE I.

The name of the corporation shall be WASHINGTON STATE CHINA
RELATIONS COUNCIL.

ARTICLE II.

The period of duration of the corporation shall be perpetual.

ARTICLE III.

(a) The primary purposes of this corporation are as follows:

(i) To unite in a common effort those persons, entities
and organizations engaged in the arts, education, communications,
labor, agriculture, industry, transportation, business and trade,
for the purpose of monitoring, facilitating, promoting, encouraging, and realizing the enhancement of relations, understanding,
goodwill and friendship between the peoples of the State of
Washington and the peoples of the People's Republic of China.

(ii) To promote the exchange of trade exhibits, educational opportunities, cultural performances and other similar
activities in furtherance of promoting friendship and understanding between the peoples of the State of Washington and the
peoples of the People's Republic of China.

-1-

(iii) To make known the unique and vital attributes of the people and resources of the State of Washington, thereby promoting the State of Washington as the natural gateway for trade, understanding and friendship between the peoples of the United States and the peoples of the People's Republic of China.

(iv) To promote and encourage the enactment of just and reasonable laws and ordinances affecting relations between the United States and the People's Republic of China, and to oppose the enactment of laws and ordinances that would be unjust and unreasonable.

(v) To provide a coordinated, unified focal point for liaison, activity, and communication with persons and entities exercising responsibility for or having interests relating to the above-stated purposes of this corporation, such persons and entities to include national, state and local governmental officials and agencies, national and regional associations or bodies, and persons or entities acting on behalf of or representing organizations or entities associated with the People's Republic of China.

(b) In addition to the above-stated primary purposes, this corporation shall have those purposes and powers authorized by the laws applicable to nonprofit corporations in the State of Washington, provided that this corporation shall not carry on any activities not generally in furtherance of the primary purposes, and provided further, that this corporation shall not carry on any activities not permitted to be carried on by a corporation exempt from federal income tax under Section 501(c)(6) of the

-2-

Internal Revenue Code of 1954 (or the corresponding provision of any future United States Internal Revenue Law).

ARTICLE IV.

This corporation is one which does not contemplate pecuniary gain or profit to the members thereof, nor distribution of dividends thereto; it is organized solely for nonprofit purposes. The property, assets, profits, and net income of this corporation are irrevocably dedicated to the furtherance of its primary and general purposes, and no part thereof shall inure to the benefit of any director, officer, member, shareholder, or individual.

ARTICLE V.

The corporation shall have no capital stock and shares thereof shall not be issued. The authorized number and qualifications of members of the corporation, the different classes of membership, if any, and the property, voting and other rights and privileges of members, their liability for dues and assessments, if any, and the method of collection thereof, shall be as set forth in the Bylaws. Certificates evidencing membership in the corporation may be issued as prescribed in the Bylaws.

ARTICLE VI.

The power to alter, amend or repeal the Bylaws or adopt new Bylaws shall be vested in the Board of Directors.

ARTICLE VII.

Upon the dissolution of the corporation, the Board of Directors shall, after paying or making provision for the payment of all of the liabilities of the corporation, dispose of all of the assets of the corporation exclusively for the purposes of the

-3-

corporation in such manner, or to such organization or organizations organized and operated exclusively for the purpose of promoting trade, friendship and goodwill between the peoples of the United States and the peoples of the People's Republic of China as shall at the time qualify as an exempt organization or organizations under section 501(c)(6) of the Internal Revenue Code of 1954 (or the corresponding provision of any future United States Internal Revenue Law), as the Board of Directors shall determine. Any such assets not so disposed of shall be disposed of by the Superior Court for King County, Washington, exclusively for such purposes or to such organization or organizations, as said Court shall determine, which are organized and operated exclusively for such purposes.

ARTICLE VIII.

Each director or officer now or hereafter serving the corporation, and each person who at the request of or on behalf of the corporation is now serving or hereafter serves as a director or officer of any other corporation, and the respective heirs, legatees, personal representatives, executors and administrators of each of them, shall be indemnified by the corporation against all costs, expenses, judgments and liabilities, including attorney's fees, reasonably incurred by or imposed upon any such person in connection with or resulting from any action, suit, or proceeding, civil or criminal, in which such person is or may be made a party by reason of such person being or having been such director or officer, or by reason of any action alleged to have been taken or admitted by such person as such director or officer,

-4-

whether or not such person is a director or officer at the time of incurring such costs, expenses, judgments, and liabilities, except in relation to matters as to which such person shall be finally adjudged, without right of further appeal in such action, suit or proceeding, to have been liable for willful misconduct in the performance of such person's duty as such director or officer. Such indemnification shall be made with respect to adjudications other than on the merits and shall extend to settlements and compromises. The foregoing right of indemnification shall not be exclusive of other rights to which such director or officer may be entitled as a matter of law.

ARTICLE IX.

The address of the initial registered office of the corporation shall be c/o Houger, Garvey & Schubert, 30th Floor Bank of California Center, City of Seattle, County of King, Washington. The name of the initial registered agent of the corporation at such address shall be Stanley H. Barer.

ARTICLE X.

The number of directors constituting the initial Board of Directors of the corporation shall be five (5) directors. The names and addresses of the persons who are to serve as the initial directors of the corporation are as follows:

Name	Address
Robert C. Anderson	General Administration Bldg. Olympia, WA 98504
Patricia Baillargeon	735 Skinner Bldg. Seattle, WA 98101

-5-

Stanley H. Barer   30th Floor Bank of
                                California Center
                                Seattle, WA 98164

James D. Dwyer   Pier 66, Bell Street Terminal
                                Seattle, WA 98111

Richard L. Kirk   1706 Seattle Tower
                                Seattle, WA 98101

Any change in the number of directors of the corporation
shall be made by amendment of the Bylaws. Election, removal and
replacement of directors shall be as provided in the Bylaws.

                        ARTICLE XI.

The names and addresses of the incorporators of the corporation are as follows:

Name   Address

Robert C. Anderson   General Administration Bldg.
                                Olympia, WA 98504

Patricia Baillargeon   735 Skinner Bldg.
                                Seattle, WA 98101

Stanley H. Barer   30th Floor Bank of
                                California Center
                                Seattle, WA 98164

James D. Dwyer   Pier 66, Bell Street Terminal
                                Seattle, WA 98111

Richard L. Kirk   1706 Seattle Tower
                                Seattle, WA 98101

DATED this ___1___ day of __August__, 1979.

                        Robert C. Anderson

                        Patricia Baillargeon

-6-

_____
Stanley H. Barer

_____
James D. Dwyer

_____
Richard L. Kirk

STATE OF WASHINGTON)
) ss.
COUNTY OF KING   )

    This is to certify that on the 1st day of August,
1979, personally appeared before me ROBERT C. ANDERSON, PATRICIA
BAILLARGEON, STANLEY H. BARER, JAMES D. DWYER, and RICHARD L.
KIRK, to me known to be the persons described in and who executed
the foregoing Articles of Incorporation, and acknowledged that
they signed the within and foregoing instrument as their free and
voluntary act for the uses and purposes therein mentioned.

    GIVEN under my hand and official seal this ____ day of
_____, 1979.

_____
NOTARY PUBLIC in and for the
State of _____, residing
at Kirkland

-7-

2

Robert A. Kapp, "Washington State Meets China," Puget Soundings, Dec. 1980
(Reprinted with the permission of the author.)

Washington state's role in the growth of our relations with China is being eagerly assisted by businesses, public agencies, and dedicated individuals who have formed an organization unique in the United States.

The United States and the People's Republic of China have entered a new era of "normalization," and Washington state has a new organization specially designed to make the most of this state's natural advantages in dealing with the PRC.

Since the two former adversaries announced the establishment of normal diplomatic relations at the beginning of 1979, the structures needed to facilitate regular international dealings have been rapidly created. An official commercial agreement followed formal diplomatic recognition; most-favored nation status was granted for Chinese imports to the United States, and, from that point, U.S.-Chinese trade has steadily improved. Meanwhile, the PRC has continued with its modernization of virtually all sectors of the Chinese economy. Despite a slower pace for costly technical modernizations in the last eighteen months, long-range development of the Chinese economy remains the centerpiece of the post-Mao regime's domestic policies. The United States, having hardly encountered the People's Republic in international trade before the mid-1970s, has now risen to third among China's trading partners, with 1980 two-way trade likely to reach four billion dollars.

The improvement of United States-Chinese relations has hardly gone unnoticed in Washington state; indeed, it could not be ignored. The state awoke to the new situation in February, 1979, when Deng Xiaoping, the energetic vice premier who has guided China to new domestic and international paths since the death of Mao, visited Seattle. The Deng visit was a festive occasion, full of talk of friendship and visions of burgeoning trade. Only three months later, the first vessel flying the flag of the PRC to call at a United States port in thirty years tied up in Seattle. Once again, Washington state played host to ambassadors and officials and newspapermen who turned out to witness an historic moment in the restoration of cordial ties between Americans and mainland Chinese.

The message was clear; good relations were once again the norm, and not-so-old enmities were on ice. The strategic implications of it all sparked debates in college classrooms and government offices; the "China Card" seemed a potent deterrent to the Soviet Union in some quarters, a risky and dangerous ploy in others. But in the Northwest and in Washington state, the heaviest concentration of interest developed around the ever-appealing but little understood China Trade.

Washington state is no stranger to trade with China; our major ports along the Pacific Coast are closer to the PRC's big harbors than any others in the continental United States; the historic presence of citizens of Chinese descent throughout the state; the stretching of rail and highway networks across the northern U.S. to link Washington ports with the markets of the Middle West—these and other factors have worked in the past to make the state the gateway to trade with the other nations of the Pacific Rim as well as with the People's Republic. After 1949, of course, U.S. trade with the People's Republic vanished. But, as relations with Beijing (Peking) gradually improved in the early 1970s, some Washington state firms began to probe markets in China again; the Boeing Company's early sale of 707 jets to China was only the most conspicuous sign of slowly developing trade ties between the Evergreen State and the PRC.

Normalization in 1979 opened new opportunities—and posed new risks. The restoration of normal economic dealings augured well for the state's role, both as a transshipment center for a nation's imports and exports and as a production center for products needed in China's modernization. Yet pitfalls remained; one of the most serious being ill-informed over-enthusiasm. In the euphoria of the early 1970s, and then again in 1977 and 1978 as China's post-Mao leadership hinted at hundreds of billions of dollars of imports from the West by the year 2000, many Americans once again fell prey to the persistent virus of blind optimism about the economic potential of the China trade. Like the trade itself, this blindness was nothing new; nineteenth-century Britishers had mused aloud about selling knives and forks to five hundred million customers, or peddling pianos to one family in five in the Middle Kingdom. Now in the 1970s, the talk was of aspirin tablets to a billion headaches and (more humorously) deodorant to two billion underarms. But the excitement was the same: with so many people in China, surely any U.S. exporter could get a slice of the action and make it big! What was needed was information and realism, not rumors and daydreams.

Here in Washington, a small group of business and government leaders who took the long view on China began exploring in early 1979 the best ways for the state to maximize its advantages in the expanding arena of United States-China relations. Trade, they realized, could not be isolated from other aspects of the new association; educational and cultural ties needed to be developed, as the people of our state and the people of China learned more about each other's outlooks and interests. What was wanted, they concluded, was a small independent organization, the sole purpose of which was the development of realistic, solid relations between the people of Washington state and their Chinese counterparts. Trade lay close to the heart of the new organization, but the whole gamut of potentially rewarding ties across the Pacific were placed on the new firm's agenda.

This new group is the Washington State China Relations Council, formally incorporated in August of 1979 and revealed to the public at the beginning of 1980. The Council's board of directors includes top executives of major firms, cultural bodies, and educational institutions throughout the state. Its *ex officio* directors include the entire Washington congressional delegation, the governor, and three big-city mayors. In the space of nine months, nearly forty Washington state companies and public agencies have joined the Council, making it the first organization of its kind in the United States—an enterprise with the strong backing, good connections, and the sole task of advancing a single state's relationships with China.

The Council's activities fall into two rough categories. First, the Council assists member firms in their dealings with China by providing information, background, language assistance, and other forms of advice. Second, the Council exposes the state and the Council's members to their Chinese counterparts and visitors with maximum effectiveness. These Chinese visitors have already included a Chinese journalist preparing to publish the first English-language daily in China since the late 1940s; the new Chinese Consul General and his wife, stationed in San Francisco and making their first get-acquainted visit to Washington state; and high-level official Chinese delegations, such as leading bankers or, most recently, Vice Premier Bo Yibo and the State Machine Building Industry Commission. Another delegation with which the Council worked closely were children's welfare and education specialists. In such cases, the Council works with national sponsoring organizations, such as the National Council for U.S.-China Trade, in Washington; or the National Committee on U.S.-China Relations, in New York. The Council keeps in close touch with these national bodies to assure Washington state's participation in important delegation visits such as these.

Above and beyond the steady flow of Chinese guests through the state of Washington, the Council seeks to make interested parties in China more aware of the state's resources and advantages. In such a vast nation, whose people often have trouble knowing the difference between the state of Washington and Washington D.C., there is a lot of work to be done, just as there is much work to do here in making China more familiar to Washingtonians. With the support of the governor, the Council is exploring a state-province relationship with a single, important province as one way of creating a special, friendly awareness of Washington state in the PRC. Increasingly, too, the Council will present Chinese language materials dealing with Washington state and our "China Connections" to friends across the Pacific.

For member firms, the Washington State China Relations Council helps to bring expert visitors, accurate information, and political and economic updates to business people and leaders who are already dealing with China or who seek to start doing so. U.S.-China trade—and technical or educational exchange, for that matter—is often a complex cross-cultural process, beset on both sides by a heavy mixture of bureaucratic sluggishness and cultural separation. The two countries have operated in different ideological and political worlds; only recently have they begun to understand how their opposite numbers do business, organize their political and economic life, and make decisions. Much is still unknown, and frequent shifts of policy or economic conditions often make even recent information obsolete. The Council keeps a finger on the flow of information from China, providing an opportunity for member firms and agencies to stay abreast of developments through periodic briefings, access to key documents, and other channels. Luncheons and other meetings with Council guests have proven popular and useful; United States Embassy officials returning from Beijing, China specialists from State Department and the Department of Commerce, and leading figures in national United States-China trade organizations have all spent time in Washington state as the guests of the Council.

With its membership continually expanding, the Council is currently establishing so-called technical committees in various special fields, such as transportation, banking, professional services, forest products, and education. Much of the Council's work will flow through the technical committees, whose members share common professional interests.

Building working ties with the People's Republic of China is not just a matter of purchases and sales; it means transferring knowledge and expertise. Training of technicians, managers, and specialists is a vital part of China's modernization effort. Washington state, with strong higher education facilities and businesses with interests in China, can participate in that vital dimension of the new U.S.-China relationship. Indeed, the process has already begun: a few of the Council's member firms have initiated on-the-spot training in their own facilities for selected Chinese personnel. The Council is well situated to help develop these important exchange projects in cooperation with its member firms.

The Washington State China Relations Council, with a staff of two and a board of directors headed by Robert C. Anderson, Director of the state's Department of Commerce and Economic Development, manages its wide range of activities from its offices in Pioneer Square, in Seattle. The office hums with efforts presently underway—and it will hum even more furiously this fall, as the Council embarks on its 1981 membership campaign. The momentum of the first exciting year of the Council is sure to continue as the Council brings its members into fuller contact with the People's Republic of China and carries the Washington state's message to increasing number of Chinese citizens.

3

William B. Abnett, Testimony at Hearings on "United States-People's Republic of China Trade Relations, Including Most-Favored-Nation Trade Status for the PRC" before the Subcommittee on Trade of the House Committee on Ways and Means, Jun. 21, 1990

(Reprinted with the permission of the author.)

Mr. Chairman:

It is my pleasure to testify today before the Subcommittee on Trade on the topic of Most-Favored-Nation (MFN) trade status for the People's Republic of China (PRC).

My organization, the Washington State China Relations Council, is a private nonprofit corporation with one basic mission: to promote and enhance commercial and cultural relations between the state of Washington and the PRC. Our Council is the *only* such state-centered association in the union. We have more than 100 members, representing businesses of all shapes and sizes—ranging from the mighty Boeing Company to the tiny "Mom and Pop" import/export firm—as well as institutions of higher learning. The Council was founded in 1979, immediately following the establishment of diplomatic relations between the United States and China. In the more than ten years since our founding, Washington state's trade and cultural ties with the PRC have flourished. Last year, our total two-way trade with China amounted to $2.6 billion—about one-seventh of *all* U.S.-China trade and more than any other state. The Council's member colleges and universities have conducted academic exchanges with scores of Chinese universities. And one of our corporate members, Northwest Airlines, has generously provided tens of thousands of dollars worth of travel grants that have supported approximately 75 scholars from Washington state in their pursuit of academic research in China.

The Washington State China Relations Council strongly urges the United States Congress to approve President Bush's waiver of Jackson-Vanik and vote to extend MFN trade status for China. MFN treatment is the cornerstone of all free and fair trade policy—in the United States as well in the General Agreement on Tariffs and Trade (GATT). America grants MFN treatment to virtually all of our trading partners, including South Africa, Ethiopia, Syria, and Iraq. In our country, MFN is *rule*, not the exception. MFN is most definitely *not* a privilege; it is the standard tariff treatment that we apply to the overwhelming majority of our trading partners. Revoking MFN status from China would not be the withdrawal of a privilege, it would be the imposition of an economic sanction—and a unilateral sanction at that. No other country in the developed world is contemplating such an action. In fact, many countries undoubtedly are licking their chops with glee, hoping that United States business—their principal competition—will be forced to retire from the China market.

The Government of the United States has extended MFN treatment to China ever since both countries established diplomatic relations more than ten years ago. Every year since then, both Congress and the President have ruled that China is in compliance with U.S. trade law regarding MFN treatment to non-market economies (Title IV of the Trade Act of 1974, Public Law 93-618), and have continued to extend MFN treatment to China. During the decade that America has been granting MFN status to China, bilateral trade has increased dramatically, from a mere $1.1 billion prior to "normalization," to a total of $18 billion last year. Moreover, strong trade ties have undeniably led to progress in other important areas of U.S.-China relations. For example, the United States has become the world's second-largest foreign investor in China, with some $4 billion of equity investment in place there. Our presence in China is significant; there are now approximately 1000 American-owned enterprises in the PRC. And as we have increased our investment in China, the Chinese have begun to invest in our country, opening scores of Chinese-owned companies in the United States during the past ten years. At present, there are at least seven PRC companies in the Seattle area, alone. Growing trade and investment ties with China over the past decade have also helped to foster greater understanding among the Chinese people of the traditionally American values of political pluralism, the free market, liberty, and humanitarianism. Only when ordinary Chinese people understand how democracy and the free market work will those ideas become reality in China.

Accordingly, the Washington State China Relations Council believes that maintaining commercial relations between the United States and China is absolutely necessary. Continued U.S.-China trade relations depend on continued renewal of MFN treatment. Removal of China's MFN status would decimate U.S.-China trade. Chinese-made products currently are subject to U.S. tariffs that average about 6 percent. If Congress were to revoke MFN treatment for China, then that country's products would be subject to discriminatory tariff rates rising in some cases to over 100 percent. These vicious tariff hikes would price many Chinese goods right out of the American market. According to private estimates, China would stand to lose at least $6 billion of its exports to the United States—about one-half of last year's total. Moreover, the Chinese would undoubtedly retaliate dollar-for-dollar against American exports to China. As our exports amounted to $5.8 billion in 1989, Chinese retaliation would virtually wipe out U.S. exports. In short, the removal of MFN treatment for China would bring an end to U.S.-China trade as we've gotten to know it over the past ten years.

In addition to having disastrous economic implications, removal of China's MFN treatment would also have dire political consequences. Bilateral political relations would deteriorate, perhaps irreparably. Inside China, hardliners would be strengthened—not weakened—by MFN removal. The hardliners would use the removal of MFN to "prove" their position that contact with the capitalist United States is not in China's interest. The fires of xenophobia and isolationism in China would be fueled, and the U.S. Government would stand to lose everything that had taken more than a decade of hard work to develop. It is difficult enough for a foreign country to influence China during a period of warm political relations, but—as we found out during the Korean War—it is impossible to do so when we are hostile to each other.

Removing MFN from China would also be a clear case of victimizing the victims—the ordinary people of China, who have suffered enough already, and are the very individuals that the American Government is striving to protect. There is no evidence that revoking China's MFN treatment would bring current regime to its knees, but there is absolutely no doubt that doing so would harm the living standards of the Chinese people. Moreover, it is a great irony that we would do the greatest injury to the most reform-oriented and entrepreneurial people in China. More than fifty percent of the products that we imported from China last year were produced in market-oriented collective factories in South China, not in Stalinist state-owned enterprises. If China's MFN treatment is revoked, the entrepreneurial collective factories—not the heavily subsidized state-owned enterprises—will be forced to shut down.

In addition to harming the pro-market reformers of South China, removing MFN from China also do grievous injury to Hong Kong, an innocent bystander and the world's last great bastion of free market economics. In 1989, fully 70 percent of American imports from China were transshipped through Hong Kong for value-added processing such as re-packaging. Removal of MFN would have dire consequences for this sector of the Hong Kong economy. Furthermore, many Hong Kong manufacturers of goods destined for the American market have moved their operations in recent years across the border to South China. Without MFN treatment, most of this business would go bankrupt. Not only would this hurt the Hong Kong economy, but it would also cause most of the approximately 2.5 million Chinese workers in South China's Guangdong Province who had been hired by these Hong Kong companies to lose their jobs. With the "1997 Question" looming so large in the minds of the Hong Kong people, shouldn't the U.S. Congress be supporting rather than undermining the Hong Kong economy?

The Washington State China Relations Council hopes that the U.S. Congress will vote to extend MFN trade status for the PRC for another year. Mr. Chairman, thank you for the opportunity to express my Council's opinion.

4

Eden Y. Woon, "China's Too Vital To Be Treated This Way," Special to The Seattle Times, Apr. 24, 1996.
(Reprinted with the permission of the author.)

"Thirty-five percent of our revenue depends on China, If China does not get renewal of Most Favored Nation (MFN) status, this will reduce severely our supply sources, thereby reducing our leverage in price negotiation with our customers. Our company would have to lay off 15 employees."—A Tacoma castings manufacturer

"Up to a quarter of out revenue depends on China. We have several offices in China conducting global logistics, with hundreds of employees worldwide involved in China business. China's our future, and removal of MFN would set us back years."—A freight forwarder based in Seattle

"One hundred percent of our revenue and our entire company's 20 employees depend on China. We are a small business which has grown substantially in the last three years. By hard work and cooperation of our Chinese partners, we are able to supply high-quality products at competitive price levels for American consumers."—An Auburn toy designer/importer

"Our exports to China have grown six-fold since 10 years ago. That represents the fastest-growing part of our business, and the trend should continue well past the year 2000. We now have a 'China' department, and virtually every existing department—purchasing, accounting, sales and warehousing—has benefited from our China ties."—A distributor of industrial tools and equipment based in Seattle

THESE testimonials of the importance of China trade do not come from large companies such as Boeing or Weyerhaeuser, whose business involvement with China has been well-documented. In terms of number of jobs, large companies' statistics are more impressive: One out of every seven aircraft built by Boeing here goes to China; 100 million dollars was the amount of revenue earned by Weyerhaeuser in China last year; and once the piracy problem is controlled, China—having the fastest PC sales growth in the world—would dwarf other Microsoft markets.

But the smaller entities mentioned above, and hundreds of companies dotting the Northwest, attest to the depth of China trade and how China trade affects many, many citizens in this region.

In the entire United States, Chinese imports benefit consumers and many importers. Across the U.S., no fewer than 200,000 jobs depend on exports to China. In Washington State, the largest export state to China, the number is large and the ratio is much higher. As I travel around this state, I have found numerous businesses either engaged with or interested in China, the fastest-growing economy of the world. Whether they are in agriculture, manufacturing, services, import, retail, high-tech, transportation, or whether they are large-, medium-, or small-sized, they have all made strategic calculations to work the China market for the next 20 years. The 100 million foreign-product consumers now in China will become 300 million in three years, and the infrastructure required to support the growth of this economy provides astounding opportunities. This is the single most important and exciting market for the Pacific Northwest for foreseeable future.

So why does the United States want to treat China as if it were Cuba, North Korea, Iraq, Libya, Burma, Vietnam or Iran? Not a day passes without some administration official or legislator rising up to threaten China about the possibility of Most Favored Nation status removed from China. Cuba, North Korea, Iraq, Libya, Burma, Vietnam and Iran are the only countries in the world that do not enjoy MFN, and we want to put China in that category.

Whatever our problems—and there are many—with China, its importance cannot be compared with these other countries. We need to get it right once and for all: That Most Favored Nation status is Normal Trading Status, available to every one of our trading partners—some of whom we have a great deal of trouble with—except Cuba, North Korea, Iraq, Libya, Burma, Vietnam and Iran.

The reasons why many want to treat China in such a disproportionate way are twofold. First, there are those who actually would love to see China being an enemy, in order to give some purpose for U.S. foreign policy in the post-Cold

War period, to argue for a bigger defense budget, and to increase U.S. arms sales to China's neighbors. Those in this camp make gratuitous statements to insult Beijing, side with Taiwan in a provocative manner, and recommend steps that will bring down the relationship. Secondly, there are those who are frustrated with the many problems in the relationship and upset with the numerous Chinese misdeeds or perceived misdeeds, and they erroneously believe that "locking China in a closet and throwing away the key" will cause China to "cry uncle" and behave.

This is a misguided policy, since the United States will be alone in this policy, not followed by Japan or any of China's Asian neighbors—including Taiwan—and not by Europe. On the contrary, all of them will rush into the economic vacuum left by the United States.

Americans will suffer. If MFN is taken away from China, prices of Chinese imports will become prohibitive—causing high prices for our consumers. China will retaliate against American exporters, and the whole relationship will plunge into an abyss. The commercial interests of the U.S. will be affected for years, as we would have no part in follow-on contracts, parts and supplies, engineering standards development and infrastructure build-up. Let us not forget about the significant strategic, environmental, trade and human-rights problems that we need Chinese cooperation on. Tough as they are to resolve now, resolving them in a post-MFN-withdrawal environment will be impossible. This is a policy to make China into an enemy; this is a "feel good" policy; but it is not an effective policy and not a policy in our national interest.

What the sensible policy toward China should be is actually very simple:

—Not only renew MFN for China this year, but renew it permanently to take this annual political grandstanding and bickering out of the front page. Threatening withdrawal makes a mockery of our credibility, and if carried out, hurts us immensely and for sure makes China into an enemy.

—Treat China as a world power by having in-depth dialogue at the highest levels of our governments—including presidential—and by developing a comprehensive and constructive framework to improve the atmosphere and substance of the relationship. Communication and trust are almost nonexistent. If Clinton can argue it is in U.S. interest to visit Russia when it is massacring Chechnyan citizens, he can argue it is in U.S. interest to visit China when it is guilty of far less.

—Then can tackle individual issues one by one vigorously as they should be. If the Chinese are guilty and U.S. law mandates, then sanctions decisions on nuclear ring magnet transfers should not be postponed. Human-rights problems and other bilateral problems frankly will have easier solutions if the overall relationship is better.

Businesses succeed in China when they first develop a good relationship with their Chinese counterpart before discussing the details of a transaction. Why can't our government take a page from our businesses' playbook and first develop a China policy that establishes a constructive framework that includes permanent MFN extension?

5

Joseph J. Borich, "Emerging China and what it means for Washington business," Keynote address at Saint Martin's College—China Business Conference, Apr. 9, 2004
(Reprinted with the permission of the author)

Why is China emerging now? What accounts for this economic and developmental boom virtually unrivaled in human history? From China's perspective, much of what we are witnessing is simply playing "catch-up."

For much of the past 2000 years of so, China was arguably—in some instances, inarguably—the most advanced nation in the world. In science and technology, commerce, social organization, governance, legal structure (including a relatively clear definition of rights and responsibilities) and education, few if any other societies could match up consistently with China over the past two millennia.

Until about 1800, that is. By the end of the Ming Dynasty, or 150 years before 1800, China had begun to turn inward, spurning its earlier progress in S&T and the advanced institutions it had created, and essentially froze in time. The "tiger" had gone to sleep. The balance shifted suddenly and dramatically to the West. By the early 1800s, the West had not only surpassed China by virtually any conceivable yardstick, it had begun to wrestle control of China's most valuable real estate away from the Qing rulers and establish foreign-run colonies on China's soil.

Over the following 150 years or so, China was beset by an almost unbroken record of disasters, natural, foreign-induced and self-inflicted. Touching on only a few of the highlights—or, perhaps, lowlights—during that period and in reverse order, we see that Chinese have had to contend with the Cultural Revolution, the famine of the early 1960s, the Great Leap Forward, the 100 Flowers Campaign, the Anti-rightist Movement, China's civil war, the Japanese invasion, the warlord period, the Republican Revolution, the Boxer Rebellion, the Taiping

Rebellion, partial colonization by western powers and the Japanese, and the Opium Wars.

All of this left China bankrupt and dispirited by the late 1970s, with a sort of collective inferiority complex and with a growing grudge against both its own leadership and its former foreign oppressors.

No wonder Chinese were ready for a new approach in 1978 when then-leader Deng Xiaoping announced the new policy of reform and opening! 25 years later, self-confidence has returned to China. Reflecting perhaps on the country's former glory as much as its bright future prospects, Chinese are now saying "It's been a rough couple of centuries, but w-e-r-e b-a-c-k!"

Starting from the late 1970s, the nation-wide policy called reform and opening has created profound structural changes in China's economy, and opened the way for a market forces in China.

It is fair to say that China's leadership did not institute the overarching policy of opening and reform for altruistic reasons, nor did its leaders experience a St. Paul-like epiphany in which they suddenly realized Marx was wrong and Adam Smith was right.

The principal motivation for this change was the realization that past excesses, in particular, the Cultural Revolution, had left the legitimacy of the Chinese Communist Party's rule very much in question. They gauged correctly that nothing less than sweeping reform of China's economy, and much more openness to the outside world would promote stability and restore the party's legitimacy.

In the past twenty five years of reform and opening as China has restructured increasingly along market economy lines, its gross domestic product has quintupled. Foreign trade has burgeoned and there has been an explosion of infrastructure development with new construction or improvements of expressways, rail lines, ports and airports, telecommunications and buildings. In 1990, there were zero miles of expressways in China; by 2010 there will be over 20,000 miles and only the U.S. will have more.

Nor is China going to let up on its torrid pace of development any time soon. The 2008 Beijing Olympiad, the 2010 Shanghai World Expo, the program to open up and modernize China's western region and the revitalization of Northeast China's industrial base will continue to play out over the balance of this decade at least, and require hundreds of billions of dollars in additional investment.

Unleashed entrepreneurship and economic development have created unprecedented prosperity for most Chinese, assuring virtually all access to the most basic human requirements of food, shelter and clothing. According to the UNDP, 200 million people were lifted above the poverty line in China between 1980 and 2000, a feat unprecedented in human history.

Rising prosperity has been accompanied by social and political change, too. The control over almost every aspect of daily life that was the hallmark of the old work unit and commune systems has been dramatically loosened. Today, Chinese have more personal freedom than ever before to decide where they will live, when and where they will travel, what they will buy, and which jobs they will compete for.

They also have unprecedented access to the world of ideas inside and outside China's borders. Today, 200,000 Chinese students are pursuing their education outside of China, many of them in the U.S. Countless more travel internationally or view the rest of the world through satellite television and the Internet.

The change China has undergone in the past two decades has not only enhanced China's stature in the community of nations and raised living standards to an all-time high, it has also engendered the longest period of unbroken social and political stability there in the last 200 years. China's soft revolution—so-called "Socialism with Chinese characteristics"—has been a great success thus far. Where does that leave China today? Although China is still a long way from fulfilling its enormous economic potential, it is already an economic superpower in most respects. At some point fairly soon, China will become the world's largest economy in terms of aggregate GDP. China already possesses one of the world's largest economies, is among the top ten nations in terms of international trade, and in 2002 surpassed the U.S. to become the world leader in attracting new foreign direct investment.

At the same time, the Chinese government is pushing ahead with an ambitious program to restructure its state owned enterprises, China's banking system and its government bureaucracy in order to make its economy more efficient and productive. And while China's economy is becoming more streamlined, its 1.3 billion consumers are becoming wealthier and more discriminating.

Further growth of China's economy will depend increasingly on domestic consumption, rather than exports and foreign investment. Retail turnover of consumer goods grew through most of the 1990s at an average annual rate of nearly 20 percent. Previously unheard of luxuries like televisions, washing machines and air conditioners are becoming commonplace. So too are private phones and home computers.

Another new phenomenon that is radically changing lifestyles in China and creating a new source of wealth is the privatization of housing. More than 80 percent of Shanghai's housing stock is now privately owned, for example, as compared to less than 10 percent a decade ago. The past seven years have seen the birth of mortgage lending, an explosive growth in the real estate market, and a dramatic increase in demand for household furniture and furnishings along with home improvement products and services. Chinese personal savings accounts now total more than the equivalent of one trillion dollars, or, about $1000 per person; how many of you have $1000 in personal savings? I know I don't!

With growing personal wealth and more freedom than ever to travel, Chinese are beginning to eye the automobile as their next major purchase. Both production and sales of cars in China are rising rapidly and China this year will move into fourth place among the world's leaders in auto manufacturing.

In addition to growing consumerism, China's economy is increasingly driven by the private sector. To encourage greater development of the private sector (for both domestically owned and foreign-invested businesses), China's parliament has passed legislation to extend to private property and investments the same protections that have always applied to the public sector. The re-emergence of the private sector as the principal engine of economic growth is vital to China's long-term goals, and is now firmly enshrined as a guiding principle of China's ruling party.

The shift toward market economics and away from state control of the economy has already come a long way, especially since the early 1990s. By now, more than 70 percent of China's GDP is accounted for by the private and cooperative sectors.

China is also becoming a major manufacturing base. Some pundits, in fact, have taken to calling China "the world's factory." While this claim is somewhat overstated, China has undeniably made use of both domestic and foreign capital and the quality and low cost of its labor force to rise rapidly among the ranks of the world's manufacturing powerhouses. It is now in sixth place and will certainly go higher.

Growth of manufacturing in China has been matched by trade displacement within Asia—i.e., Japan, South Korea, Taiwan, and others have shifted production, including production for exports, to China.

Much of what China exports are labor intensive products such as toys, footwear and textiles. As China's share of the U.S. market for such products has grown to over 60 percent in the last decade, so has Taiwan's, South Korea's and Hong Kong's combined share declined by roughly the same amount.

Thus, while our trade deficit with China is mushrooming into uncharted territory, our overall trade deficit with Asia is actually declining as a percentage of our global trade deficit.

Higher-end products for export such as computers are for the most part assembled rather than manufactured in China. The sophisticated guts of these products are largely manufactured outside of China, then put together, encased and (somewhat misleadingly) labeled "Made in China" by low-cost Chinese workers. In fact, over half the value of China's imports and exports is accounted for by this kind of export processing.

We may anticipate, however, that China will move toward manufacturing and exporting its own higher-end, higher value products. We should also expect more original technologies and designs coming out of Chinese enterprises and laboratories. In fact this is already beginning to happen in cutting-edge areas like information technology and bio-technology. With China now graduating as many engineers per year as the U.S., this trend will certainly accelerate.

But, foreign investment, technologies and management will continue to play a significant role in China's development for quite some time to come. Foreign invested enterprises have accounted for much of China's capital expansion, attracted unprecedented levels of both domestic and foreign investment, and helped create millions of new jobs.

As we have seen, much of the growth in China's exports and manufacturing over the past decade has been accounted for by foreign invested enterprises. In fact, nearly fifty percent of what China exports globally is actually produced by foreign invested enterprises.

Nevertheless, to reach its full economic potential China will have to do more to develop international markets for its own brands and products, as Japan, Taiwan and South Korea have already done successfully. This it seems to me would be the next logical step in China's rise as an economic superpower.

Lest we think that China's march to modernity and economic superpowerdom is without its speedbumps, we'd best think again. What are some of the issues facing China today? Number one is the sheer size of its population.

With a land mass roughly the same as the U.S.' China contains nearly one-fifth of the world's population. Imagine for a moment the U.S., but with China's population: a California with 160 million people, or a Washington with 30 million, or a greater Seattle with about 15 million. Those are the kinds of numbers we'd be talking about, if the U.S. had the same population as China's. And you think traffic is bad here now!

Moreover, although China's birthrate is declining, the population will still likely reach about 1.6 billion by mid-century when growth is expected to level off. What this means is that China will still grow by the equivalent of Japan's population in about a decade, and by the equivalent of the U.S.' within a generation.

Despite remarkable growth and development, China's economy remains fragile in many respects with great disparities between various regions and sectors.

China's economy will strain to meet the rising demands of its population. Just to soak up first time applicants entering the job market, China has to create about

10 million new jobs each year. Like the U.S., China must also struggle with the effects of economic restructuring that has resulted in the loss of tens of millions of urban jobs over the past decade.

In industry, too much of China's capital and labor remains locked up in the state owned enterprise system. Although restructuring has helped many of these enterprises become more efficient and even profitable, they are by and large still protected from competition, and continue to enjoy ready access to operating capital through unrecoverable loans from state owned banks. This artificial skewing of capital allocation means that the private sector, which is the only economic engine in China currently generating new jobs, often goes begging for investment capital. China has another problem that the U.S. put behind it a century ago: the rationalization of agriculture. China still has about 400–500 million people engaged in farming—mostly subsistence farming. This accounts for over a third of its population. Despite the fact that about 100 million peasants abandoned farming and moved to the cities in the 1990s there are still far too many farmers eking out a living on plots of land averaging less than an acre. Urban planners in China are predicting another 200 million farmers or more will migrate to the cities this decade, possibly overwhelming urban economies and services.

Why is all of this important to us?

Earlier in my talk I stated that China is already an economic superpower. Clearly, though, it is one with still-enormous unfulfilled potential. That is the reality of China today, a country that economically has made the right moves so far and is well into the process of self-transformation into a mighty economy with all the market and private enterprise bells and whistles so loved by westerners. That said, however, we must acknowledge that the transformation is no where near complete, and more work still lies ahead. What then does all of this mean for doing business with China?

Just looking at basic data, it is easy to understand why the U.S. Department of Commerce attaches such overriding importance to this, the very largest and most promising of the world's big emerging markets.

It is a nominal market of 1.3 billion people. Even discounting the portion of the population engaged in subsistence agriculture that still leaves hundreds of millions living in or near metropolitan areas, and with growing disposable incomes. Over one-third of these urbanites would qualify as middle class or higher based on purchasing power parity calculations.

On top of that, China's economic growth rate, though slightly slower than during the 1990s, is still likely to be among the world's highest in this decade.

There are opportunities for foreign firms in virtually every sector of the economy, from providing expertise and capital equipment to meet China's infrastructure needs, through supplying industrial equipment and materials to China's booming industries, to retailing consumer goods and services for China's burgeoning middle class. I would single out environmental protection as a particularly promising sector. Nearly a quarter of the US$ 26 billion China will invest in the 2008 Beijing Olympics is earmarked for environmental protection and cleanup, for example.

On top of that, China can provide a wide range of quality products at competitive prices to foreign buyers.

It is still, and will remain, a major supplier of textiles, apparel, footwear, foodstuffs, machinery, metals and metal products, chemicals, raw materials, electronics, toys, games, sporting goods and handicrafts. Increasingly it is also a source for high-end products and equipment as well.

In Washington State, the leading export to China by far, of course, is transportation equipment, especially aircraft. However, China offers a major and growing market for many of this state's products, including agricultural products and food, information technology equipment and services, forestry products, and environmental technology. Washington businesses looking to enter the China market must balance the tremendous potential of that market against the daunting barriers to success.

As numerous businesses have already demonstrated, firms can succeed in the China market, but success is often slow in coming and usually not easy to achieve. The China market is not El Dorado, and it is not for the risk averse.

Despite all of the reform and opening, China still sees itself as a socialist state ruled by a communist party. While this philosophy of governance is changing over time, it is important to remember that China is not yet a capitalist society, or an entirely free-market economy, and should not be thought of as one by those seeking to do business there. Other problems that may hamper foreign business include a weak banking system and generally underdeveloped financial institutions; a still-confusing and sometimes opaque system of regulations and laws governing business, often administered inconsistently; and transportation bottlenecks, to name but some.

My purpose in enumerating these difficulties is not to discourage prospective trade and investment with China, but to draw attention to the challenges one must face and surmount in order to succeed. Given these challenges, a commitment to doing business in China must be firm and long-term.

There, I hope I've provided a bit more perspective on the subject of today's conference. But, I can't resist the temptation in closing to offer some hopefully useful, based on my own experiences and the wisdom I've gleaned from others over the years.

1. **Due diligence is as important in China as anywhere else.** It is more difficult to perform in China, but not impossible. The myth that Chinese business is opaque and impenetrable is just that—a myth. Which leads directly to the next tip:

2. **Get professional help.** There are now many reputable, reliable firms in China—both Chinese and foreign—to assist with due diligence and also provide legal, real estate, accounting and market research services. Find and use them.

3. **Choose the right partners.** Whether you are investing or trading, you will need agents, distributors, customers, and suppliers. Invest the time and energy to know them well before making commitments. Good partners won't guarantee business success, but bad partners will ensure failure. Want to simplify matters by employing the services of a reputable "middle man"? Fine, but don't put all your China business eggs in one basket. Get to know all the major players in your supply or marketing chain.

4. **Take a long-term view of the China market.** Hang on to that long-term focus as you encounter the inevitable problems that come with doing business in China. Your strategy can't be based on the quarterly P&L statement. But, your China business plan needs a reasonable time horizon, too (example).

5. **Be flexible.** You will need creative solutions to deal with the dynamic conditions of China's market, and to meet the challenges created by China's

legal and regulatory structure. Be prepared to compromise on your tactics, but not on your basic strategy and core principles.

6. **Don't be afraid to say "no."** Your products may be too advanced or not price-competitive in the China market today. You don't necessarily need to jump in now in order to ensure your competitiveness 3–5 years from now.

7. **Pay attention to "guanxi,"** the Chinese word loosely translated as "relationship." We tend to form business relationships for business reasons. Personal relationships may or may not follow business relationships. In China (and in Confucian cultures generally), the tendency is for business relationships to grow out of personal relationships. Take the time to cultivate a <u>network</u> of mutually supportive personal relationships.

8. **Visit frequently.** It takes time and a demonstration of personal interest in China to investigate the market and find the right partners. It takes even more time and personal interest to cement relationships with your partners.

9. **Be culturally aware.** Learn at least a few polite phrases in Chinese. Acquire an authentic Chinese name of two or three characters and use it on your business cards. Don't plan trips to China around local holidays there. Do sample the food offered you, but don't ask what it is until after you've sampled it!

Much of the above may sound like common sense, but it's amazing how often common sense is forgotten or ignored by foreign companies in their eagerness to get their business going in China.

Finally, let me wrap this up with a few words about the Washington State China Relations Council.

The Council a 25-year old private non-profit organization whose mission is to serve our member companies and, in general, promote commercial, cultural and educational ties between this state and China.

Our 150 member corporations and organizations represent every sector of the economy, as well as cultural and academic interests. What all of our members share is a strong interest in China.

Although we are not government-funded, we work closely with the Washington State Government, the U.S. government, and local governments throughout China to promote our members' interests in China.

We offer business consulting services, including contact building and assistance with resolving business disputes. We will soon be able to offer a full menu of professional consulting services with the assistance of several of our member firms.

We also organize a variety of programs every year to help build better understanding of China and how to do business there. Among our planned major events this year are:

- A conference September 8–9 in Seattle with leading Chinese and American economists, government officials and business leaders to discuss Sino-American economic relations;
- An environmental conference October 19–21 in Seattle with 80 Chinese environmental professionals to discuss China's environmental problems and opportunities for Northwest environmental companies; and
- A special program on November 10 in Seattle with the executive director of the Shanghai 2010 World Expo Organizing Committee to highlight business opportunities that are available to U.S. companies as Shanghai prepares for the 2010 Expo.

If you are doing business with China, or planning to do business with China, you might wish to consider joining the exclusive community of WSCRC-member companies. For more information please visit our website at www.wscrc.org.

Thank you!

6

Program cover of the Council's 25th anniversary gala

Celebrating the 25th Anniversary of the
Washington State China Relations Council
1949 1950 1951 1952 1953 1954 1955 1956 1957 1958 1959

1960 1961 1962 1963 1964 1965 1966 1967 1968 1969 1970

1971 1972 1973 1974 1975 1976 1977 1978 1979 1980

1981 1982 1983 1984 1985 1986 1987 1988 1989

1990 1991 1992 1993 1994 1995 1996 1997 1998

1999 2000 2001 2002 2003 2004 年6月18日...

Milestones in a Partnership
Brought Together by the Trade Community

Appendix B

Council Red-Letter Dates—Chronology

Aug. 6, 1979	Articles of Incorporation are filed at the Office of Secretary of State of the State of Washington.
Nov. 2, 1979	Robert A. Kapp agrees to accept the position of Executive Director.
Jan. 3, 1980	Council announces its formation at a news conference in Seattle.
Apr. 19, 1980	First quarterly newsletter is published and sent out to 17 Council members.
Sept. 1, 1980	Chinese Vice Premier Bo Yibo visits Seattle and praises the Council.
Oct. 1, 1980	Kapp turns full-time.
Jun. 25, 1981	First Council delegation in Sichuan to develop state-province ties between Washington State and Sichuan Province.
Oct. 11, 1982	Governor John Spellman and Governor Lu Dadong sign agreement in Chengdu formally establishing relations of friendship between Washington State and Sichuan Province.
Aug. 1, 1983	First five awards announced of the Council Travel Support Program made possible with a gift from Northwest Airlines, which was renewed through 1990s.
Sept. 13, 1983	Sichuan Governor Yang Xizong returns visit to Washington State.
Nov. 4, 1983	First Council annual conference "China Trade Update" convenes.
Apr. 19, 1984	Council briefs President Ronald Reagan at headquarters of Weyerhaeuser Company, a member, in Federal Way.
Summer 1984	Membership tops 100.
Oct. 19–27, 1985	Kapp accompanies Governor Booth Gardner to China, including meeting then Chinese Vice Premier Li Peng.
May 21–23, 1986	Chinese Vice Premier Yao Yilin visits Washington State, with the Council arranging his activities.
Spring, 1987	Executive Committee decides that it is lawful for the Council to lobby the U.S. Congress.
Jan. 1987	Membership reaches 130.
Jul. 1, 1987	William B. Abnett becomes Executive Director.
Apr. 15, 1988	USTR Clayton Yeutter speaks to the Council.
Jun. 4, 1989	Tiananmen demonstration crackdown shakes U.S.-China relations and the Council.

Nov. 29, 1989	Douglas H. Paal, China advisor to President Bush (41), speaks at the Council's seventh China Trade Update conference.
Jun. 21, 1990	Abnett testifies for China's MFN before the Subcommittee on Trade of the House Committee on Ways and Means.
Nov. 28-Dec. 1, 1990	U.S.-China Symposium and Exposition on Industry, Technology, Trade and Economic Cooperation convenes in Seattle without the Council support due to uncertainty over China's MFN.
Dec. 1991	With membership and revenues declining, the Council eliminates position of program associate and contracts management with WCIT (Washington Council on International Trade).
Apr. 1992	Kapp begins serving concurrently as Executive Director of the Council and President of WCIT.
Nov. 20, 1993	APEC (Asia Pacific Economic Cooperation) summit opens in Seattle, with Kapp playing a pivotal role bringing it here.
Dec. 1, 1994	Eden Y. Woon becomes Executive Director, with membership at 57, an all time low.
Oct. 30, 1995	William J. Perry, Secretary of Defense, speaks at the Council luncheon, dismissing "China as a threat."
May 29, 1996	Anson Chan, Chief Secretary of Hong Kong, speaks to a breakfast co-sponsored by the Council on the 1997 transition.
Oct. 1996	Council gets its first homepage at http://www.eskimo.com/~wscrc.
Jan. 1997	Membership reaches 180, an all time high.
Aug. 1997	Joseph J. Borich becomes Executive Director
Oct. 12–14, 1997	Governor Gary Locke's first trade mission to China with Borich as his China advisor.
Nov. 15, 1999	U.S. China Bilateral WTO Agreement is signed.
Nov. 19, 1999	Council holds discussion on the Agreement with Wang Yunxiang, China's Consul-General in San Francisco.
Nov. 30-Dec. 3, 1999	WTO Ministerial Conference in Seattle. Council and the US-China Business Council give joint reception to Chinese delegation headed by Shi Guangsheng, Minister of Foreign Trade and Economic Cooperation.
Oct. 10, 2000	President Bill Clinton signs into law the bill granting China Permanent Normal Trade Relations status.

Apr. 1, 2001	EP3 spy plane takes emergency landing in Hainan, China, casting uncertainty over U.S.-China relations.
Apr. 18, 2001	Darryl Johnson, Deputy Assistant Secretary of State for East Asian and Pacific affairs, speaks to the Council on the incident.
May 4, 2001	Chinese Ambassador Yang Jiechi speaks to the Council on U.S.-China relations and the incident.
Aug. 2001	Council annual banquet features Ambassador Joseph W. Prueher, a vital player in ending the spy plane crisis.
Dec. 11, 2001	China becomes a member of the WTO.
Sept. 28, 2002	Council decides to take new initiatives and provide more trade-specific services to members and non-members.
Oct. 11–18, 2003	Borich helps arrange and joins Governor Locke's third trade mission to China, the most successful one, resulting in millions of dollars in sales for Washington state business and agriculture.
Jun. 18, 2004	Gala celebration of the 25th anniversary of the Council is held at the Bell Harbor International Conference Center in Seattle, featuring Ambassador Clark T. Randt, Jr.
Feb. 2005	Council debuts Consulting Services Group.
Jun. 2005	Membership over 150 and steady.

Appendix C

Council Makeup and Growth—Membership Then and Now

Council Membership (1980)

The Boeing Company
China Arts Corporation
China Products Northwest
Concrete Technology Corporation
Container Services, Inc.
Coopers & Lybrand
Crane, Stamper, Boese, Dunham & Daily
Crane & Crane, Inc.
Davis, Wright, Todd, Riese & Jones
Emery Air Freight Corporation
Ernest & Whinney
EST Industries, U.S.A., Inc.
Foster, Pepper & Riviera
Garvey, Schubert, Adams & Barer
ITT Rayonier, Inc.
John Fluke Manufacturing Co., Inc.
Johnson & Higgins of Washington, Inc.
Kerr Steamship Company
Key Tronic
Marsh & McLennan, Inc.
McGregor Land & Livestock Company
Northwest Airlines, Inc.
PACCAR, Inc.
Pacific National Bank of Washington
Pacific Northern Oil
Pacific Northwest Bell
Peoples National Bank
Perkins, Coie, Stone, Olsen & Williams
Physio-Control Corporation
Port of Seattle
Port of Tacoma
Preston, Thorgrimson, Ellis & Holman
Puget Sound Power & Light Company
Rainier National Bank
Sax and MacIver
Schoenfeld Industries, Inc.

Seattle-First National Bank
Seattle Stevedore Company
TRA
United Airlines
University of Puget Sound
Washington Iron Works
Washington Public Ports Association
Washington State University
Way and Brockman
Weyerhaeuser Company

Council Membership (2005)

(Partial)

Outstanding Members

Fluke Corporation (Electronic Testing and Measuring Devices)
Microsoft Corporation (Computer Software)
MulvannyG2 Architecture
PACCAR International (Truck & Mining Equipment Manufacturers)
Port of Seattle (Marine and Air Transportation)
Port of Tacoma (Marine Transport)
The Boeing Company (Aircraft, Aerospace)
Weyerhaeuser Company (Forest Products)

Sustaining Members

Columbia Machine, Inc.
Costco Wholesale (Consumer Goods)
Dan Terry & Associates, Inc. (Design Engineers & Manufacturers of Aluminum Extrusion)
Davis Wright Tremaine LLP (Law)
Dorsey & Whitney LLP (Law Firm)
Ederer LLC (Port Cranes and Hydropower Construction Equipment)
Expeditors International (Freight Forwarders)
Garvey, Schubert & Barer (Law)
Heller Ehrman LLP (Law Firm)
KPMG LLP (International Accounting and Tax Services)
Northwest Airlines
Perkins Coie LLP (Law)
Port of Everett (Marine Transportation)
Preston Gates & Ellis LLP (Law)
Russell Investment Group (Global Investment Management Firm)
Skyway Luggage Co. (Wholesale Luggage Manufacture and Distribution)
SuperValu International (Grocery Import/Export)
U.S. Bank (Banking and Financial Services)
Washington Mutual Bank (Banking and Financial Services)
Washington State Department of Community Trade and Economic Development
Wells Fargo HSBC Trade Bank N.A. (Banking and Financial Services)

Contributing Members

APAC Host International Inc (Consulting, Tour & Conventing between China & USA)

Bank of America (Banking and Financial Services)

China Pacific Group, Inc (Consulting Services)

COSCO North America, Inc. (Shipping Lines Agency)

Genie Industries (Industrial Equipment Manufacturing)

Impex Development L.L.C. (Import/Export)

Jesse Engineering Co. (Metal Fabrication and Machinery Manufacturers)

Magna Force, Inc. (Mag-lev Transportation)

Medtronic Physio-Control (Medical Equipment)

North America Industrial Investment Co., Ltd (Investment, Acquisition/Mergers Financing)

Pacific Northwest Advisors (Consultants)

Regal Financial Bank (Bank)

Sheraton Seattle Hotel & Towers (Hotel)

Starbucks Coffee Company (Coffee)

Vanson HaloSource (Health Science)

Members

Aegis Medical (Medical Personnel & Consulting)

Almax Sales Company (Electronics Broker & Representative)

Asia Pacific Professional Services & Language School (Translation and Language Services)

B.A.T.L. (Technical Documentation & Customer Support)

BC Pacific Inc. (steel and metal fabricators)

Bellingham Cold Storage Co. (Consulting on Domestic & International Matters)

Callison Architecture (Architecture)

Certech International, Inc. (Environmental Consulting/Product Marketing)

ChappelWang PLLC (Law Firm)

Charles Schwab Global Services (Financial Services)

Crane International Inc. (Consultants)

Cross-Cultural Consulting Services (Cultural Consulting/Graphic Design)

Esterline Corporation (Specialized Manufacturer, Aerospace/Defense)

Evergreen Produce, Inc. (Agriculture)

Factory Assurance & Qualification, LLC (Consulting on production/quality control)

GH Associates (Security Consulting)
GMI (Integrated Global Market Research Services)
High5 Sportswear Inc. (Distributor and wholesaler)
Imperial Garden Seafood Restaurant (Restaurant)
Industrial Distribution Group (Wholesale Distribution)
Kentridge (USA) Inc.
Key Technology, Inc. (Machine Vision System Mfg.)
L & L Financial Services (Mergers and Acquisitions)
LIYA International, Inc. (Trade Services/Professional Exchange Delegations)
M. Brashem, Inc. (Import/Export Distributors)
Mera Technologies, Inc. (Manufacturing)
MutualNet International Inc. (International Trade & Convention Services)
Nelson Irrigation Corporation (Agricultural Equipment)
Neural Techs Business Information Incorporated (Business Intelligence)
Newport Technologies (Wireless/telecom market development in China)
Northwest Laboratories (Dental Laboratory)
Northwest Products Inc (Imports/Website)
Pacific Bamboo Resource Group, Inc. (Bamboo products and supply resource mgt.)
Pacific Valley Foods
Pacifica Bank (Bank)
Porter Novelli (Public Relations)
Rittenberg Associates Inc. (Consulting)
Robert A. Kapp & Associates (China Strategy, Business Consulting)
Schwabe Williamson & Wyatt, P.C. (Law Firm)
SeaTab Software
Sharpe Mixers (Engineer/Manufacture Industrial Mixers)
Speckman Law Group PLLC (Patent Law)
State of Alaska, International Trade, Office of the Governor (Trade Promotion)
Teragren LLC (Manufacturer, Building Products Made From Bamboo)
The Hanlin Moss Group, P.S. (Certified Public Accountants, Valuation Analysts)
UPS Supply Chain Solutions, Inc. (Full Service Transportation Logistics)
ZF International (Chinese Art Importers)

Non-Profit Members

America's Foundation for Chess (Friendship through competition with China)
Central Washington University

City University (Education, degrees & certificates)
East Gates International
Kent Chamber of Commerce
Northwest Horticultural Council (Tree Fruit Industry Association)
Pacific Lutheran University
Pacific Northwest National Laboratory
PATH (Program for Appropriate Technology in Health)
Rural Development Institute (Research Institute)
Seattle Art Museum
Seattle Chinese Garden Society
Seattle Community College District (Education)
Seattle-Chongqing Sister City Association
Snohomish County
South Puget Sound Community College
St. Martin's College
University of Phoenix (Accredited College & Graduated Level Education Inst)
University of Puget Sound (National Liberal Arts College)
University of Washington
Virginia Mason Medical Center
Washington Council on International Trade (Trade Policy)
Washington State Potato Commission (Director of Trade & Market Access)
Washington State University
Western Washington University
Whitman College
Whitworth College (Education)
World Affairs Council Seattle
World Association for Children and Parents (Child Adoption Services)
World Trade Center Tacoma

Closing Note

Writing this book has been a labor of love, a love for the ever dramatic and ever growing relations between the U.S., my adopted country, and China, my homeland; a love for those who have made it their career or business improving the relations; and a love for all who care about China.

It has also been a discovery, a discovery of "hidden dragons and crouching tigers," not as the movie title but in its original sense as a Chinese proverb of the same words—hidden heroes of unusual abilities. To me, the founders, directors and presidents of the Washington State China Relations Council are such heroes among us.

I thank all who encouraged and helped me with this project, Mr. Joseph Borich first of all, Mr. Robert Anderson, Ms. Patricia Baillargeon, Mr. Stanley Barer, Mr. James Dwyer, Mr. Richard Kirk, Mr. Robert Kapp, and Mr. Eden Woon. I thank again Messrs Kapp, Barer and Borich for agreeing to evaluate this maiden book of mine. I thank those presidents who took time out of their busy schedule or retirement to write those precious comments. I thank Mr. Bruce Ramsey, editorial writer of the Seattle Times, for copy-editing the final draft on very short notice. I thank last Mr. William Abnett for the date to attend the Council's 25th anniversary gala that gave me the inspiration to write this book.

Wendy Liu
October 2005

An Update: Established at 30

With the blink of an eye, five years have passed since the summer of 2004 when I decided to write this book. This past September, the Washington State China Relations Council held its 30th annual banquet. This year, 2009, also marks the 30th anniversary of the normalization of U.S.-China relations.

"Be established by 30," Confucius said, even though the ancient philosopher was talking about milestones in an individual's life. However, just as it is for an individual, Big-Three-O is also a major milestone for the Council. Also as with an individual, more maturity comes with more challenges, too, especially in "this economic downturn," as Mr. Joseph Borich said recently.

Yes, Borich is still there. After serving as the executive director for 12 years, the longest term in the Council history, Borich is now president. Along with him, serving as the board chair, is Dennis Bracy, chairman of Avatar Studios, a multimedia production company with operations in China.

Thanks to my on-going contact and correspondence with Borich, I have kept up with the development of the Council over the past few years.

New priority

In 2002, after China's accession to the WTO, the Council began to reprioritize its work. Instead of promoting ties between Washington state and China or lobbying for China's normal trade status, the Council has emphasized services to its members, especially oriented toward their commercial interests in China.

By mid 2005, the Council had started working on two programs in that direction. One was the Consulting Services Group, conceived to serve both member and non-member clients in their specific business needs in China.

The other was China Business Planner, an annual conference, organized to help members and other participants with their China business plans for the following year.

Although the programs were discontinued after a two-year trial run, the idea behind them, Borich said, has continued. In 2008, the Council formed an alliance with a company in Shanghai to bring Chinese business opportunities to Washington state, especially to member companies. The Council has also run a number of less formal programs in the same spirit, along with its more regular programs such as the executive director's public speaking engagements, the public education program, member information services, and members' forum.

Hu in town

One event, however, may have overshadowed all others in the past few years: the visit to Seattle by Chinese President Hu Jintao on April 18-19, 2006.

Even though it was former Washington Governor Gary Locke who played the instrumental role in making the visit possible, the Council, Borich told me, was on the committee organizing the visit. Working alongside him was Council President Nelson Dong, a partner of Dorsey & Whitney LLP, with extensive Greater China experience. Council members were also major facilitators of and participants in the event.

By visiting here, President Hu highlighted once again the special status Washington state enjoys in U.S. relations with China, a status the Council had helped build over the years.

How special was that status? Let me count the ways: 1. For his first state visit to the U.S. as the Chinese president, Hu came to Washington state first instead of Washington, D.C; 2. For his only dinner event in the U.S., Hu was at Bill Gates' house instead of the White House; 3. To give a good example, at a public luncheon, of a win-win outcome of U.S.-China trade, Hu pointed to The Boeing Co.; 4. To show the popularity of an American product in China, Hu said he used Microsoft's Windows every day; 5. To propose a toast to Sino-American friendship and mutual benefits of good relations, he used Starbucks coffee served in a Starbucks mug.

Further emphasizing that special status, President Hu said to his hostess, Governor Chris Gregoire, that he did not choose to visit Seattle only because it was the closest major U.S. city to China, but also because Washington state enjoyed close and fruitful exchanges and cooperation in economy, trade, education, health, science and technology with his country.

Clean energy

The best illustration of those close and fruitful exchanges between Washington state and China in recent years is the U.S.-China Clean Energy Forum, which Borich said was the result of the conflation of two initiatives related to the Council.

One was by Washington Sen. Maria Cantwell, a director ex officio of the Council. With the reputation as an envionrmental champion, Cantwell was also continuing the tradition of the late Sen. Henry M. Jackson in terms of China relations. While visiting China in November 2006 with a Council-assisted delegation, Cantwell called on the U.S. and China to promote energy cooperation, rather than competition. She later called the relationship "coopetition." She invited China's National Development and Reform Commission (NDRC) to begin a dialog in Seattle with its U.S. counterparts to create a framework.

Another initiative was by a Council member company, the law firm Garvey Schubert Barer—the same Barer who was a founder of the Council. The firm, with the Council's assistance, was trying to introduce to the China market Northwest companies specializing in clean and renewable energy technologies, products and services with an exchange forum called "the Smart Energy Exchange Project with China."

By spring 2007, the two initiatives merged to become the U.S.-China Clean Energy Forum. In mid-September that year, the Forum was officially launched in Beijing, with the visit by U.S. members of the joint preparatory committee and their counterparts at the NDRC and other stakeholders in China.

What exactly is the mission of the Clean Energy Forum? Borich explained it this way to Council members in his October 2007 newsletter:

> "The goal of this process is not about adopting any particular form of technology, but rather creating an ongoing conversation among private and public sector leaders from the two countries to focus on removing impediments and facilitate cooperation. It is designed to put an intense focus on how we can translate good intentions into near-term action."

That mission was put in the "MEMORANDUM OF UNDERSTANDING: Cooperation on Clean Energy And Alternative Fuels" signed in Seattle in March 2008. Representing the American side was Stanley Barer, national co-chair of the U.S.-China Clean Energy Forum. Representing the Chinese side was Co-Chair Han Wenke, director general of Energy Research Institute under NDRC.

With that, the Clean Energy Forum was firmly established. Its CEO was none other than Dennis Bracy, the Council chairman. A number of meetings have followed since, culminating in the May 2009 meeting in Beijing, which adopted a list of eight priority initiatives, from establishing a joint energy lab to creating a smart grid, and commercializing solar technology and electric cars.

With the Obama administration holding a dialog with China on clean energy in February 2009 and signing a MOU on U.S.-China cooperation on energy, climate change and environment in July 2009, it is clear that the Washington State China Relations Council is once again at the forefront of U.S.-China relations as a convener, organizer, promoter, and above all, a bridge.

New vision

After attending the Council's 30th anniversary banquet, I went to see Borich, this time at a different location than five years ago. With the current economic situation, the Council had cut expenses and staff and moved into a smaller office.

But, having worked from Taipei to Shanghai, Mogadishu to Seattle, and with all the ups and downs in the Council history over 30 years, Borich remained upbeat and optimistic. In fact, he revealed to me a new vision he and Bracy shared for the Council as well as Seattle.

With Washington state's pioneering role and special status in U.S.-China relations, with the Council leaders and members spearheading the clean energy cooperation between the United States and China, they believed that Seattle had the potential to someday be the Davos of U.S.-China relations.

Davos of U.S.-China relations! Wow!

It is not easy for the Washington State China Relations Council to reach 30. But who would have thought it could be this exciting looking beyond 30?

There will always be highs and lows in the life of an organization or an individual. But vision is what makes a difference. It was a vision that brought the Council into being in 1979. It was a vision that sustained the Council in the aftermath of Tiananmen in 1989. It was a vision that steeled the Council through the anti-WTO "Battle in Seattle" riots in 1999. It will be the new vision that would strengthen the Council in 2009 and onward—the vision of making Seattle the "Davos of U.S.-China relations."

Why not?

Wendy Liu
November 2009

Author with Joseph Borich, President, WSCRC,
at the Council's 30th annual banquet, Sept. 24, 2009

Dennis Bracy (r.), Chairman, WSCRC, with William Stafford (l.),
President, Trade Development Alliance of Greater Seattle

With Robert Anderson and Stanley Barer,
founders/former presidents, WSCRC

Borich with Clark T. Randt, Jr., American Ambassador to China
(2001-09), and Gao Zhansheng, Consul General of China
in San Francisco

43077269R00150

Printed in Poland
by Amazon Fulfillment
Poland Sp. z o.o., Wrocław